PRAISE FOR

Which Way Is Up?

"With a warrior's strength and a mother's tenderness, Susan Chapman takes us on her cancer journey, from the paralyzing grip of fear to the open expanse of love, framed by the traditional bardo teachings. This is a compelling book."

—IRINI ROCKWELL, author of *The Five Wisdom Energies*

"In this tumultuous age of global uncertainty, *Which Way Is Up?* invites us to dive deep down into our collective heartbreak in order to resource from the fertile and regenerative depths of meditation practice. Susan Gillis Chapman offers steadfast compassion, grace, clarity, and a generous invitation for growth. She supports the reader each step of the way, as she offers the medicine of seeing and perceiving more clearly, from the heart, as an alternative to feeding fear, reactivity, and overwhelm. She invites us to come home to peace with our ever-changing world and human experience and to move from a fear-based response to freedom of the heart."

—DEBORAH EDEN TULL, author of *Luminous Darkness*

"Enlisting the basics of contemplative psychology, Susan guides her readers into embodied listening, the discovery of innate bravery, and the capacity to strengthen compassion in the face of real challenges. This book offers compassionate wisdom—directly from the heart—and will benefit anyone undergoing groundless times."

—MELISSA MOORE, author of *The Diamonds Within Us*

"This book is like a wise old friend accompanying us in the most difficult of times. Susan Gillis Chapman goes right to the heart of our deepest fears, sharing her own story in a way that sheds light on our greatest moments of suffering and invites us to allow the journey to be transformative. She offers clear practices and insights that serve as signposts to guide the reader through difficulty with compassion and fierce love."

—HALA KHOURI, author of *Peace from Anxiety*

"When Susan received a cancer diagnosis during the isolating years of the pandemic, she was able to draw on her years of Buddhist training for support. In this book, she shares the insights and practices that sustained her in dealing with the initial shock of the diagnosis and throughout the challenges of treatment. It is a great resource for anyone going through an abrupt or startling transition in life."

—JUDITH L. LIEF, author of *Making Friends with Death*

"Forged by the fires of direct experience, and buttressed by decades of deep meditative practice, this is a profound and practical journey of the heart crafted by a spiritual warrior. Susan Chapman deftly translates the Buddhist teachings on the bardo into language you can understand and immediately apply to the challenges of life. If you want to learn how to transform obstacle into opportunity, this book is for you."

—ANDREW HOLECEK, author of *Reverse Meditation*

Finding Heart in the
Hardest of Times

WHICH

WAY

IS

UP?

SUSAN GILLIS CHAPMAN

SHAMBHALA

Shambhala Publications, Inc.
2129 13th Street
Boulder, Colorado 80302
www.shambhala.com

Cover art: redchanka/stock.adobe.com
Interior design: Kate Huber-Parker

9 8 7 6 5 4 3 2 1

First Edition
Printed in the United States of America

Shambhala Publications makes every effort
to print on acid-free, recycled paper.
Shambhala Publications is distributed worldwide by
Penguin Random House, Inc., and its subsidiaries.

Library of Congress Cataloging-in-Publication Data
Names: Chapman, Susan Gillis, author.
Title: Which way is up?: finding heart in the hardest of times / Susan
Gillis Chapman.
Description: First edition. | Boulder, Colorado: Shambhala Publications,
Inc., [2024] | Includes index.
Identifiers: LCCN 2023029398 | ISBN 9781645472131 (trade paperback)
Subjects: LCSH: Self-actualization (Psychology) | Mindfulness (Psychology)
Classification: LCC BF637.S4 C4862 2024 | DDC 158.1—dc23/eng/20230802
LC record available at https://lccn.loc.gov/2023029398

To Jerry

CONTENTS

CONTENTS

WHICH
WAY
IS
UP?

Introduction

Anxiety, heartbreak, and tenderness mark the in-between state. It's the kind of place we usually want to avoid. . . . The challenge is to let it soften us rather than make us more rigid and afraid. Becoming intimate with the queasy feeling of being in the middle of nowhere only makes our hearts more tender.

—Pema Chödrön, *The Places That Scare You*

T his book was born during the COVID-19 pandemic when a friend said to me on a Zoom call, "We use so many different words for it, but there is one thing we're all dealing with: fear."

I agreed. Words streamed through my mind: *anxiety, trauma, concern, worry, panic, uncertainty, nervousness.* In the past, I'd sometimes joked that my credentials as a contemplative psychotherapist came not so much from my graduate degree but from being an expert in fear. As a teenager I learned to ride the kind of horse that bucked me off regularly. My adult life was a similar bumpy ride. So, fear is something I'm very familiar with. But then again, aren't we all?

The 2020s is unfolding as a decade driven by fear. It began with a global pandemic that forced us into isolation behind closed borders, lockdown restrictions, and masks. Even the most ordinary of exchanges, such as with our grocery clerks, were blocked by plexiglass. Behind those barriers, we also had our individual crises. Mine began in the summer of 2020 when I was diagnosed with triple-negative breast cancer (TNBC), a rare, aggressive, and hard-to-treat form of the disease. In the months that followed, my personal experience sensitized me to the difficulties other people were going through behind their masks. That winter our family lost a loved one to the opioid epidemic. Friends had their homes destroyed by wildfires and floods. In the background, hateful speech was spreading like a virus through our social and political conversations. As I write, the devastating war in Ukraine is raging. And above all, our climate crisis is worsening. It feels like we're in a collective free fall but are so overwhelmed that we can't even get oriented as to which way is up! This helpless feeling of disorientation is a human emotion everyone can relate to during hard times.

If we were left with fear alone, we could never survive difficult times in our lives. Thankfully, there's another human experience that has the power to absorb, embrace, and transform these challenges: love. Love also goes by many names: kindness, generosity, gratitude, mercy, tenderness, understanding. When love in any of its forms comes together with fear, the roots of our human nature are nourished. This is because we're like trees in a forest. From the view above the ground, it may appear that we stand alone, but below the surface we're interdependent, always in relationship. When those roots are nourished, we have an inner strength that enables us to reach beyond ourselves and help each other. We're connected to a social supply chain that delivers ordinary acts of courage and resilience.

Having cancer during the pandemic lockdown brought home to me how challenging it can be to keep an open heart when you feel paralyzed by fear. Fear is a crisis of trust. If we lose trust in the power of love, it will trigger us to shut down, freeze our hearts and minds, and build walls between us. This misguided path leads to the worst of human suffering.

In my life I've been fortunate to be guided by teachers from contemplative Christian, Zen, Shambhala, and Tibetan Buddhist traditions who showed me how to work with fear. Their instructions were like shock absorbers for riding the energy of disruption rather than getting bucked off. I've worked with these teachings as a meditation practitioner, a therapist, and a Buddhist teacher for decades, but when my personal life fell apart with my cancer diagnosis, I had a chance to test them out with life itself on the line.

DARK NIGHT OF THE SOUL

I've written this book coming from a few different perspectives: as a patient who suffered her own rude awakening, as a Buddhist practitioner, and as a family therapist trained in contemplative psychology. Contemplative psychology is an approach to understanding the mind that includes both Western and Buddhist psychology. The starting point for healing others is being in relationship with our own suffering by practicing meditation. This book uses my cancer story as an example of the kind of crisis that Buddhists refer to as a *bardo*, which is described in more detail in the next introductory section. It's a transitional period of radical change. For some of us, the bardo shows up as a dark night of the soul, a spiritual crisis. For others, it might be more practical, such as a period of unemployment or a divorce. But for most of us, it's simply a feeling of things falling apart.

Left on our own, we might feel hopeless, frozen by fear. The teachings in this book are a guide that can meet us there, inviting us to hold steady in the present moment. Paying attention and being willing to listen is the gift of loving-kindness, an inborn capacity of our human heart to melt the barriers between us. In your own times of change or hardship I hope these instructions will help you engage in a process of healing and discovery. While this book draws from Buddhist teachings as a framework, you don't have to be a Buddhist practitioner to benefit. Rather than being religious, this path is a contemplative approach, a way of understanding our mind through the lens of meditation and self-reflection.

HOW TO USE THIS BOOK

Your bardo journey has a beginning, a middle, and an end, which are represented as part one, part two, and part three in this book. Each chapter within these parts offers a way to work with fear as a stepping-stone from one stage to the next.

Part one is about how to work with the initial groundlessness of a bardo. It focuses on what I call "awake fear" and how to manage it by learning to listen to your body in various ways. Part two, the middle of your journey, meets the challenges of "frozen fear" with compassionate wisdom. And part three, the end of the bardo journey, shows you how turning inward to meet your deep-seated "core fears" can lead to a new beginning or metaphorical rebirth.

Each chapter concludes with a practice section to help you self-reflect on your unique situation and to delve deeper into the teachings. Each practice section comprises a contemplation and a meditation.

Contemplations

This book uses examples from my personal contemplative journal to encourage you, the reader, to create your own. The teachings here on meeting fear with love are primarily from the Buddhist tradition, but all spiritual traditions share similar themes. Anyone who is willing to turn inward, to listen to music or poetry and feel their heart, is already attuned to this inner path.

I invite you to join me in working through our bardo journey together, the one you are in now or the one that waits around the corner. The practice section at the end of each chapter begins with a contemplation. Each invites you to reflect on the chapter's teachings in your contemplative journal and consider how it applies to your life. A contemplative journal is more than a diary; it's a place to record the kind of self-reflection that invites a deeper understanding of the events in our lives. All you need is a notebook. Instead, you might want to record your reflections in a voice memo on your phone, or you might prefer to meet and discuss each chapter with one or two friends.

Contemplative practice is like a diving board. First, you climb the ladder by bringing to mind some of the key points you've just read. Repeat those key points slowly to yourself. Then imagine going to the edge of the board and diving into your personal experience, letting go of stories and thoughts and listening to your own wisdom.

Pause, feel, breathe. Don't judge or compare; just welcome how the meaning behind these words feels right now. Before writing in your journal, always listen to your body. Breathe, create space. Feel the sensations in your body, feel the energy moving through without freezing into thoughts. Then write your self-reflections in your journal.

Meditations

A central tenet of Buddhism, as well as other contemplative paths, is to awaken insight with the threefold practice of hearing teachings, reflecting on them, and then listening to our own experience directly in meditation. The ideal way to learn meditation is in person or in a retreat setting, but the meditations in this book are short and accessible enough for you to try on your own at home. I'd recommend you set aside five or ten minutes for these, but please feel free to adapt my suggestions with whatever contemplative and meditation practices work best for you.

In general, it's recommended to meditate in a seated position, on a chair or cushion, in a relaxed but upright posture. Some people find it helpful to record the instructions on their phone and play them back as a guided meditation.

The topic of fear is triggering, I know. If at any point along the way you come to a dark place that's too hard to navigate in this way, as I did from time to time in the past few years, I encourage you to reach out to a professional counselor or spiritual guide for support.

At the same time, I am confident that the information I'm passing along to you from my teachers can be helpful if you're seeking a healing spiritual path during difficult times. These instructions meet the challenges of our personal bardos, allowing these times of fear to make us more compassionate and resilient. Like trees bending in a storm, when our roots go deep, we can meet our emotional storms without breaking.

Thank you for joining me on this journey as we move, one step at a time, on a path of learning to listen to our bodies, our hearts, and each other. The bardos of our lives can be times of spiritual awakening and personal transformation. But they are also the hardest times of our lives. So, take care, and let's proceed slowly, gently, and with love.

Welcome to Your Bardo

Most people have come to prefer certain of life's experiences and deny and reject others, unaware of the value of the
hidden things that may come wrapped in plain or even ugly
paper. In avoiding all pain and seeking comfort at all costs,
we may be left without intimacy or compassion; in rejecting
change and risk we often cheat ourselves of the quest; in
denying our suffering we may never know our strength or
our greatness.

—Rachel Naomi Remen, *Kitchen Table Wisdom*

The three words *you have cancer* stopped my mind. I didn't hear
anything after that. I was on my mobile phone, sitting on a park
bench. My husband, Jerry, had wandered off alone, and I saw his
silhouette in the distance. I was flooded by sadness as I imagined a
future without me at his side. In that first moment, the word *cancer*
felt like a death sentence. My rational mind knew that this wasn't
necessarily true, so why did that word trigger such a shock? Nearly
fifty years earlier, I began practicing meditation in response to the
sudden death of my younger brother in a car accident. Since then,
I've contemplated the inevitability of death almost every day. So
why did this diagnosis pull the rug out from under me?

A PERFECT STORM

Having cancer during the COVID-19 lockdown felt even more catastrophic. A silent killer was growing in my body, and I was heading into unknown territory. Within days of my diagnosis, a team of medical experts swung into action, mapping eight months of treatment with surgery, chemotherapy, and radiation, plus another year to recover. All this in the science fiction–like isolation of the pandemic. I would never see the faces of my doctors, nor anyone else's, because they were hidden by masks. Without greeting each other, patients would drift by in the hallways of the cancer center like ghosts and land silently apart, socially distanced in the waiting rooms. I realized there was a word for the black hole I found myself in, and it wasn't *cancer*. With this diagnosis, my world had turned upside down. I had fallen into a bardo.

THE BARDO

Finding the word *bardo* was like being handed a flashlight in a dark tunnel. It reminded me of the instructions that could illuminate my path forward. While the medical team was treating the cancer in my body, these bardo teachings could heal the suffering in my mind and heart.

A bardo is usually not the kind of experience we enter by choice. It's a rude awakening. In Tibetan Buddhism, this term is used to describe the transition period between death and rebirth. But in my graduate studies in contemplative psychology, my fellow students and I were trained to apply these teachings to any gap that disrupts what we think of as our normal life when our past disappears behind us and our future expectations dissolve before our eyes. It could be a fender bender on our way to an important interview or the gaping hole in our heart when our teenager moves away from home.

I studied and practiced these bardo teachings during the nine years I was in a Buddhist retreat at Gampo Abbey, Pema Chödrön's monastery in eastern Canada. Previously I had worked as a therapist, creating a safe listening space for people in crisis. It wasn't until my cancer diagnosis that I was able to see how these two sets of experiences fit together.

The Tibetan Book of the Dead is the best-known source of original teachings on the bardo. Throughout the book, the key instruction is "Please listen!" The same is true in a therapy office. A counselor is trained to pay attention and listen, and this is the skill we teach our clients. "Please listen to your body, to your heart, to what you are about to say. Please listen to each other!" We use the word *listen* as if listening is an ordinary activity, but from a contemplative perspective, being able to authentically listen is a profound skill. It's the ability to create space, to let go with an open mind and heart. Listening is the key to liberation in a bardo, including those times in our life when our world turns upside down.

WORKING WITH FEAR, FINDING SUPPORT, AND EMBRACING LOVE

Learning to listen is an essential instruction, but what voice are we listening to? When someone is dying, a spiritual friend might say, "Don't be afraid." We might hear that voice but what do those words mean?

The crises in our lives trigger all kinds of emotional reactions: anger, grief, raw irritation. But underneath them all is fear. If we can learn how to work with fear, the other emotional reactions won't destabilize us. But how do we do this? Fear isn't the kind of experience you can simply delete on command.

The Buddhist teachings give us a voice we can trust when we're on shaky ground, overwhelmed by fear. Using my personal journey as an example, I hope I can offer you the kind of support you need for whatever crisis you're going through. During the initial shock of my cancer diagnosis, I was handed a list of dos and don'ts to prepare for the treatment protocol. But more than anything, the bardo teachings provided the map I needed for the emotional journey ahead.

There is one emotion that's more powerful than fear: love. In the absence of love, fear can turn toxic. But when embraced by love, the fear that arises in our bardo can be transformative. Like fear, love has many faces and names. Love is a stranger lending a helping hand when we stumble on the sidewalk. Love is also our own impulse to be that helper. Love is a child smiling at us over her father's shoulder in line at the grocery store, and love is the spontaneous response we give back to that child. Love is a friend who brings a meal to our doorstep when we're grieving, and love is the gratitude that pays that kindness forward to someone else. Opening ourselves to love highlights the flow of ordinary kindness that's always been there, nourishing us in the background of our lives.

THREE BARDO STAGES

The traditional Buddhist approach to the after-death bardo describes three stages. In each stage, a spiritual friend guides the deceased person by talking them through the fearful experiences unique to that stage. Throughout, we're urged to please pay attention and listen. In this book, I'll adapt those three stages and offer Buddhist teachings to support the crises we go through in our lives. The circumstances may be different, but the emotional landscapes have a lot in common.

Beginning: Mindfulness and Loving-Kindness

The first stage of a bardo is the shock of unexpected loss. Whatever we considered normal suddenly disappears. It's a kind of death, a sudden shift and loss of our familiar routine. This might be the moment you receive a diagnosis, split up from a long-term partner, lose a job, or anything else that shakes up your life significantly. The friend we need in the beginning is someone who can tell us the truth, who can be present with us. In part one, "Find Direction in Awake Fear by Listening to Your Body," we will take our first steps in our bardo journey, focusing on how to find that friendship in our own body with mindfulness and loving-kindness.

Middle: Compassionate Wisdom

The middle stage of a bardo is a period of hallucination when our mind plays tricks on us and our emotions react wildly. This is what happens when the habit of denial sets in after the initial shock of a bardo. Denial freezes communication between our body, heart, and mind. When we close our eyes to the truth of impermanence, interdependence, and the flow of our present-moment perceptions, we latch on to unexamined opinions that offer a false sense of security. For instance, we might want to ignore our diagnosis or punish ourselves for the ending of our relationship. We might get lost in retaliation fantasies after being laid off from our job. We need to not only hold our pain but also unmask these self-deceptions. In part two, "Meet Frozen Fear with Compassionate Wisdom," we focus on how to listen to our heart, cultivating compassion and wisdom so that we can learn how to work with the thoughts and emotions that pull us away from the truth of our present-moment reality.

End: Rebirth

The final stage of a bardo is when we're propelled to take rebirth. This is our topic for part three, "Move from Core Fear to Compassionate Rebirth." The Buddhist teachings tell us that there are two different currents in a bardo that determine what our new normal will look like. We're driven by either fear or love. When fear rules, our choices are shaped by the force of mindless habit. We're motivated to seek rebirth in familiar comfort zones, which are not safe at all. In the Tibetan Book of the Dead, a spiritual friend will try to interrupt this trajectory by reminding us to take a closer look at where we're heading. In our adaptation of these teachings, we can learn to be that spiritual friend to ourselves by gently extending our attention to the part of ourselves that is afraid to look at our core fears, the doubt we have about our own basic goodness. This allows us to take the alternative path to rebirth that is motivated by love and compassion. Every time we turn toward our fear with gentle acceptance, we're strengthening the power of compassion. This is how the suffering of our bardo crisis can be transformed into wisdom for the benefit of others. Many people who have survived a tragic loss, a "dark night of the soul," or a cancer journey describe this transformation as a deeper understanding of the meaning of love.

WARRIOR TRAINING

Preparing for a journey through the bardo is a spiritual warrior training. We're not going to battle in an aggressive way, but we're learning to be brave by facing our fears instead of covering them up. By envisioning the bardo as a journey—with a beginning, a middle, and an end—we have an opportunity to disarm fear in all its forms. At first we meet the fears that are vividly present, like shock or panic. But we can also discover those fears that are masked or hidden in the background. Like playground bullies, those fears only have power because we're too afraid to turn around and look them in the eye. The practice of a spiritual warrior is to be willing to meet our fears, confusion, and suffering with an open mind and heart. But to do this, we need the kind of support that this guidebook aspires to offer.

It's good to remember that these transition periods in our life don't last forever. The truth of impermanence—the understanding that all in existence is temporary—is hard to hear when things are going well in our life, but it's a comfort when we're having a hard time. There will be a dawn at the end of the darkest night. At the same time, keeping the bardo instructions in mind during difficult times will give us an opportunity to see our fears exposed in a way that allows us to work with them.

Contemplation

DEFINING YOUR BARDO

- What is your personal version of a bardo?
- Describe the following phrase in your own words: "that sinking feeling when our past disappears behind us and our future expectations dissolve before our eyes."

Meditation

JUST REST, DO NOTHING

10 MINUTES

This meditation is a practice of letting go and simply resting. It's giving ourselves space to just be present, here and now.

Sit in a chair or a cushion and simply rest in this present moment. No need to do anything; just welcome whatever you are feeling right now.

Notice the way thoughts pull you to the past or future. Just notice this, no need to stop them. This welcoming space is ground zero, the first gift you can offer yourself in a bardo.

The Three Faces of Fear

In order to experience fearlessness, it is necessary to experience fear. The essence of cowardice is not acknowledging the reality of fear. Fear can take many forms.

—Chögyam Trungpa, *Shambhala:*
The Sacred Path of the Warrior

Years ago, my family traveled to Nepal to meet a Buddhist meditation master, Tulku Ugyen. Every morning before sunrise, we'd hike up a steep hill and enter the stone steps of his dark, unheated monastery. We were escorted up to the third floor where we would wait for him to give us teachings.

One morning, we were sitting on the floor at the foot of his bed, and the sun was rising behind him. It was the perfect situation I'd always dreamed of. We'd climbed the mountain, met the great guru, and now we waited for the profound instruction. He said a few opening words and then looked directly at each one of us. "You are going to die. Your death is right around the corner. Your death is so close," he said as he pinched his fingertips together. "It's like the width of a horsehair; it's around the corner from you, right now. You are going to die." He repeated it eight or nine times. Then when he had our attention, he said gently, in almost a whisper, "Please don't waste your time."

We were stunned. Shortly after, we left the monastery and walked in silence down the path. Finally, Jerry turned to me and said, "Gosh, you know, for just a moment there, I thought maybe I would die someday." We cracked up, because we realized that the teacher was not only waking us up but also pointing out how quickly denial sets in.

WAKE-UP CALL

For many people, the path of spiritual warriorship begins with the shock of realizing that death is real. After the initial impact of this truth, we try to remind ourselves as often as possible because it's easy to drift back into numb complacency. The reality of impermanence is more than the reminder about death. Our circumstances can change without warning—for instance, when a romantic evening ends in a fight or when you break your leg on a ski vacation.

Some people don't really hear the words "You will die" until they have only weeks left to live. People I've met in hospice tell me that accepting the inevitability of death makes every moment precious. They don't want to waste their time, and they seem to intuitively know what emotions to let go of and what to nourish. They may be sad, but their hearts are full of love, gratitude, and mercy.

THREE KINDS OF FEAR

Sometimes fear wakes us up; at other times, it shuts us down. To meet the challenges of a bardo, the strength we need comes from being curious about fear rather than letting it push us around. What are the fears in the background of our minds that trigger us to go into denial? These three kinds of fear seem to occur instantaneously, but there are important differences that we can learn to identify.

1. Awake Fear

Awake fear keeps us safe. It wakes us up when our cell phone accidentally goes off in the theater and snaps us to attention when a truck lurches toward us on the highway. Awake fear is an intelligent message from reality. Without thinking, we know what to do.

I was awakened by fear when I heard the teacher's words: "You will die." It was like an emotional seismograph, an undeniable message from reality. *Open your eyes and see what is true.* At the beginning of our bardo journey, the instruction is to stay open to the shock of awake fear and keep listening to reality. The way to do this is to cultivate mindfulness and learn to listen to our body, something that will be discussed more in part one.

Awake fear is one of the many responses that arise from the intelligence of our heart when we're listening openly to our present-moment reality. It protects us by interrupting distractions. It brings us back to our senses so that we can be more embodied here and now. It awakens our natural empathy so that we respond to other people with sensitivity. This intelligence is an inborn capacity we all have. But without training in mindfulness, the window for staying awake is usually brief.

2. Frozen Fear

After hearing the truth from my teacher, I noticed how quickly the habit of denying death set in, like a carjacker seizing control of my mind. This denial is an example of *frozen fear*, our topic for part two of the book. Rather than connecting us, frozen fear isolates us from each other, turns us away from the present moment and silences our own intelligence. In the Buddhist tradition, frozen fear is *ignorance*, the root cause that creates the illusion that there are walls that divide us from each other, triggering chain reactions of hatred, addiction, or greed. We experience this sense of isolation as a mindless impulse to defend ourselves at the expense of our relationship with others. When this barrier is up, we're not able to listen, hear, or pay attention.

Ignoring reality isn't a safe option, especially when we're in a crisis. But frozen fear is a habit we learned long ago. Denying the truth takes a lot of energy. We're frozen in place, recycling old reactive patterns in our mind even though they cause harm. It feels so familiar that we think of these defensive habits as essential to our survival. We even think of them as who we are.

3. Core Fear

The third kind of fear is at the core of this false defensive identity. This is what triggers us to shut down when we feel vulnerable. *Core fear* is a chronic anxiety that lurks somewhere in the background of our mind—a fear that we're not worthy, not lovable, or not good enough. This self-doubt is barely reachable behind the layers of our defensive patterns.

In my previous book, *The Five Keys to Mindful Communication*, I describe how this core fear is exposed in a bardo situation: "In-between is a place we normally don't want to enter. We find ourselves there when the ground falls out from beneath our feet, when we feel surprised, embarrassed, disappointed—on the verge of shutting down. At this moment, we might feel a sudden loss of trust, an unexpected flash of self-consciousness."[1]

Core fear causes us to hide our vulnerability by spinning a false identity out of these self-deceptions. To move toward a new beginning, we'll reckon with core fears in part three.

It's worthwhile to clarify the differences between these three kinds of fear because we don't have the vocabulary in the English language to describe the nuances of experience that are central to Buddhist psychology. For instance, awake fear is one of a range of emotions that are attuned to our present-moment reality. In my work as a contemplative therapist, I've referred to these as *green light* emotions because they are trustworthy examples of emotional intelligence. Any information we receive from the present moment will update our preconceived ideas so that our actions can be more appropriate to the situation we're in.

In contrast, frozen fear, or denial, overrules the truth of the present moment and diverts emotional energy into reactions that inevitably make our situation worse. The more attention we give to the justifications and story lines that support these reactions, the more at risk we are for causing harm to ourselves or others. We don't have to look far into the consequences of hatred, jealousy, or addiction to know what this means.

The value of isolating core fear, or background anxiety, is that it turns our attention to the central teaching of the Shambhala path[2] of spiritual warriorship: the truth of our basic goodness. These teachings point out that doubting our goodness is the root cause of all the other forms of suffering we experience from turning away from fear. The idea of core fear is not unique to a spiritual path; it's familiar to many applications of psychotherapy. Here, in the context of our path through the bardo, it is presented as a way to transform our sense of identity when we experience groundlessness so that we can give birth to a greater sense of authenticity.

Contemplation

EXPLORING YOUR RELATIONSHIP TO FEAR

· Reflect on and write about your personal examples of the three kinds of fear:

- awake fear
- frozen fear
- core fear

Meditation

WAKING UP

10 MINUTES

Telling ourselves the truth about death is also the truth about the preciousness of being alive. Allow yourself some time to feel the impact of this teaching.

Sit comfortably. Imagine that you're visited by a loved one who has died. Visualize this person in front of you speaking to you: "My dearest, please understand how precious your life is. Death is real; it can come without warning. This isn't bad news. It's my gift to you. Please remember."

Feel how these words land in your heart. Repeat them in your own words. Stay present with whatever emotions arise. If you like, you might want to place one or both hands on your heart.

Embarking with
a Boundless Mind

There is a quiet light that shines in every heart. It draws no attention to itself, though it is always secretly there. It is what illuminates our minds to see beauty, our desire to seek possibility, and our hearts to love life.

—John O'Donohue, *To Bless the Space Between Us*

The day after Tulku Ugyen's teaching on death in Nepal, I visited a neighboring monastery to formally renew the bodhisattva vow. When I originally took this vow, years earlier, my teacher described a bodhisattva as someone willing to relate to our tenderness. This vulnerability feels like a sore spot, a gap in our armor that lets our basic sanity shine through. Taking this vow committed me to grow this embryonic compassion in a lifelong practice of opening the heart as a spiritual warrior. I decided to retake this vow because of an experience I had the previous week while walking down one of the dusty roads near Kathmandu. A child was begging by the side of the road. I took one glance at his twisted, broken legs and then turned away, feeling overwhelmed and powerless. I thought, "I can't handle this!" Then a spontaneous experience occurred to me. I felt as if I was holding the child in my arms and soothing him. In my mind, I said to him, "It may take infinite lifetimes, but I promise someday I'll personally make sure you'll be free." At that moment, I felt as though this boy was no different from my own child. I have no idea if there really are future lifetimes or if I would ever have the kind of power I was wishing for. But the effect of that sudden irrational thought was that it interrupted the urge to look away and allowed me to gaze into his eyes even though, at the time, I had nothing to offer him.

This was a memorable experience. At first I couldn't look at this child because it was too painful for me to see his broken body. But then I looked into his eyes, for a moment, and made a mother's promise. That's when I realized how practical the bodhisattva vow to liberate all beings from suffering can be. It is a reminder that love is more powerful than fear, and on that day, it gave me the courage to open my heart instead of turning away. The lesson I took away from that experience was this: If the bodhisattva vow enables me to turn and face the suffering of a child that I normally couldn't bear to look at, this is a path I can trust. There wasn't anything else I could do on this Nepalese road at the time, but I later learned of a program that rescued and educated many of these abused children, and I've been able to support it.

When my Buddhist teacher Chögyam Trungpa introduced me to the path of the bodhisattva warrior, his instruction was "Don't rely on my words; the teaching will emerge as you learn to face your own fear." At the time I felt that fear was something to be ashamed of. Now I realize that without it, there would be no stepping-stones for the path ahead.

MEETING TARA

At the end of the bodhisattva vow ceremony, walking in a slow line to receive the teacher's blessing, I turned and found myself face to face with a life-size statue of Tara, a female Buddha symbolizing our own enlightened potential for compassionate wisdom. I'm a visual learner, so it helped me to remember what the features of Tara represented. She sits on a lotus, signifying that fearlessness blossoms from the mud of our own confusion and fear, not from anywhere else. She holds a flower that is said to blossom at night, with a fragrance to help those lost in the dark to find their way home. The statue had a brilliant diamond eye in the middle of her forehead, a reminder of the wisdom that sees the truth of our basic goodness. As with all Buddhist deities, Tara is not an external goddess to worship or supplicate; she is symbolic of our human potential. Following the path of spiritual warriorship, it's possible to cultivate these qualities in our hearts, which in turn could help liberate ourselves and others from fear.

For an instant on the road with the begging boy, I had a flash of what the mother love of Tara feels like. The path of awakening the heart is inspired by images like this that mirror our capacity for limitless love. We can also appreciate examples of ordinary people who meet their life crises with extraordinary compassion and wisdom.

The bodhisattva path is the ongoing practice of not turning away. The bodhisattva vow is the intention to stay in relationship with everyone and every situation you meet, and to listen openly with a loving heart. Though it's a lofty aspiration, bravery doesn't come from applauding our successes but from opening up to our failures. Each step of this path exposes our hidden fears. We must meet these fears with compassion because most of us have the wrong idea of what love is. We cling to positive feelings and want to reject discomfort. Tara symbolizes an unconditionally loving heart that's bigger than all of this. These wisdom teachings are paradoxical: we come home to unconditional love not by looking to receive it from outside ourselves but by finding it to be the true nature of our own boundless mind and heart.

As with many ancient traditions, Buddhist teachings are delivered in words, parables, and symbolic images. The path of working with fear is sometimes described as the story of a lost child being reunited with a loving mother, an image that came to life for me in a vivid way with the begging boy on the road. In the Tibetan tradition, Tara, the liberator from fear, is one example of this mother. Another example is Prajnaparamita, the mother of all Buddhas, who symbolizes the space and openness of our inborn wisdom. In the bardo teachings, the union of mother and child is said to be possible at the moment of death when we finally recognize our true nature, our primordial innocence. These two aspects of our human experience—the lost child of fear and the embrace of love—are the key ingredients of our spiritual path. In this book, we will explore this relationship as a way to melt the frozen fear that divides us from our own heart.

While episodes of groundlessness occur from time to time along the way, the path itself is our own life story. Using the symbolism of the mother and the frightened child, we can reauthor our story to better understand the loving goodness of our true nature.

The teachings in this book focus on the three stages of a bardo, the three kinds of fear, and how to meet each step of our journey with bravery, turning toward our heart instead of away.

Mindfulness and Loving-Kindness

At the beginning of a bardo experience, we might feel like a lost child, fearful and in need of the loving presence and support of other people. When our life seems to fall apart, the image of a mother represents the teachings on how to stay awake by accepting change rather than denying it. When we see the truth of impermanence, the loving presence of others can reignite the pilot light of courage in our heart.

Compassionate Wisdom

In the middle of a bardo, the mother figure manifests as compassionate wisdom that shows us the truth of our interdependence with each other. This is a supply chain of kindness that nourishes us. As if seeing through the eyes of a wise grandmother, we begin to unmask the self-deceptions that justify cutting ourselves off from others and melt the frozen fear that depends on the habit of turning away.

Rebirth

Though it may seem eternal when we're in the midst of it, our bardo crisis will indeed eventually come to an end. We'll be reborn into a new normal, and that rebirth will depend on how transformative our dark night of the soul has been. To some degree or another, the light at the end of our own tunnel will soften us, inspiring us to go back in with a torch to help others find their way. Like a wounded healer, we've made the journey and understand from experience how to meet the suffering that others are going through. This is being reborn into compassionate action, bringing our intention to be there for others into our everyday life.

BEGIN WITH OURSELVES

To become more emotionally resilient in a bardo, you don't need to become a Buddhist or take the bodhisattva vow. These instructions can be followed by anyone interested in a contemplative life. The qualities of love and wisdom we're cultivating are human, not divine. I would never have found this path had I not met my teachers— exceptional human beings who proved that it's possible to open our hearts beyond limits, extending unconditional warmth to everyone, even our enemies.

It's important not to mistake these instructions as bypassing compassion for our own pain. The key point is that it's only by listening and making a relationship with our own suffering that we find our shared roots with others.

From the chapters in my contemplative journal, you will hear variations of the story of fear being embraced by a loving mother. I hope this inspires you to discover how this path opens in your own life, especially during those tumultuous times when you feel lost in the dark.

Contemplation

SELFLESS LOVE

- You don't need to be female or a biological mother to experience the kind of selfless love symbolized by Tara. Write about an example that comes to mind, such as the image of rescuers risking their lives after an earthquake, trying to save the life of a person they've never met.
- Reflect on your own experience of selfless love.

Meditation

OPENING OUR HEART

10 MINUTES

Love without clinging has a lonely quality of sadness along with a sense of spaciousness. When we listen carefully to our heart, we can discover this feeling of tender sadness in the very first moment, before any other emotion arises. Training with meditation gives us the clarity to turn our attention to that first moment, before our stories carry us away. We don't need to fix what might not be broken. This tender sadness isn't something to be afraid of; it's the true nature of our heart.

(continued)

Meditate on loving-kindness, with the feeling of unconditional love that a parent has for a child. Repeat the following wish in your own words, allowing time for it to take root in your mind and heart: *May I and all beings be happy; may we be safe and at peace. May we always be in the company of friends and family who support us with love and understanding. May we be healthy in body, heart, and mind.*

Loving-kindness is the wish for limitless health, happiness, peace, safety for ourselves and others. Ask yourself, "What does this love feel like?" It doesn't matter what the object is. It could be a beautiful flower, a playful child, a beloved pet.

What would it be like for this ripple effect of love to expand outward, to include friends, strangers, and enemies?

Pause and breathe.

How does this feel in your body right now? Let go of stories and come back to this feeling.

Find Direction in Awake Fear by Listening to Your Body

The healing of our present woundedness may lie in recognizing and reclaiming the capacity we all have to heal each other, the enormous power in the simplest of human relationships: the strength of a touch, the blessing of forgiveness, the grace of someone else taking you just as you are and finding in you an unsuspected goodness.

—Rachel Naomi Remen, *Kitchen Table Wisdom*

T he first phase of a bardo is the shock of sudden change. We've just lost our job, a loved one has died, or we're hit with depression. This is a time when we need a friend to remind us to stay awake with fear, not to turn away.

AWAKE FEAR

In the traditional teachings on the bardo, when a loved one has died, the first thing to do is validate their experience, tell them the truth. You stay in relationship with your loved one, speaking to them as if they have taken off on a journey but your bond is not broken. "You have died; I'm here for you, pay attention, and don't let fear overwhelm you." Applying this teaching to our own experience, when a sudden change occurs in our life we can stay awake with the fear that arises by meeting it with compassionate presence.

My family doctor is this kind of friend. A week after my biopsy, I visited her to get the pathology report. "Your tumor is triple negative, an aggressive cancer that will require surgery, the strongest chemotherapy regime, and radiation," she explained. I tried to keep my composure. I'd done some research and was sure that I was out of range for this diagnosis, which, sadly, most often strikes young women of color.

Then, breaking through her typically professional demeanor, my doctor softened the blow. She leaned forward and held my hand. "Don't worry, sweetheart, we will do this together. We've caught it early. You're strong. The next year will be tough, but you can do it."

What my doctor offered wasn't a cure but the compassionate presence I needed to stay awake with my fear. In a bardo, we need a friend like her—someone who will gently tell us the truth without suppressing or exaggerating the facts of our situation.

LOVING PRESENCE

My doctor did more than read me a report. She told me the truth in a tenderhearted space that was bigger than my fear, a space that telegraphed the message "I see you; I feel you; I'm here with you. We're going to be in this together." Hearing this, my initial panic subsided without turning off wakefulness.

When our life has been disrupted, when we hear shocking news, we need this kind of loving presence to make sense of our new reality. We need a friend who is willing to step away from the hectic pace of normal life and simply sit quietly with us so that we can stay present in the free fall of this new bardo. To avoid shutting down, we turn to a friend who validates our experience, as if holding up a mirror.

In this and the following chapters of part one, I will introduce you to an unlikely friendship that we can rely on to help us stay awake with fear: the relationship with our own body.

THE BODY'S TRUTH

Our body is always telling us the truth. Life is impermanent—we are born, we get sick, we grow old, and we die. Along the way, there is beauty, joy, and love. For many of us, our body has been like a lost child disconnected from our natural home, Mother Earth. We've been occasionally cruel, dissociating from our body and judging and blaming that part of ourselves as if it were an object: "Too fat." "Too slow." "Not tall enough." "Not good enough." All along, our body has been here, grounded in the present moment, ready to show us the ordinary magic of what it means to be alive.

For me, cancer and the truth of death awakened a determination to finally inhabit this body before I lose it altogether. I realize that I have no idea what my body really is because my body isn't an idea. It's an experience.

31

1

Stillness

Learn to be alone. We do not go into the desert to escape people but to learn how to find them.

—Thomas Merton, *New Seeds of Contemplation*

Because I live in Vancouver, a city at risk for "the big one," we regularly get instructions for how to survive an earthquake: "Your instinct is to run for the door, but the best thing to do is to simply drop to your knees, go under a table if you can, and hold steady." This is also good advice for a bardo. When the ground suddenly shifts under our feet, our habit is usually to look for the nearest escape. It isn't easy to simply hold steady, not knowing what will happen next.

Like an earthquake, our bardo crisis begins as a sudden jolt, and the shift it makes in our lives will change us forever. It can be shocking, frightening, bringing grief and trauma in its wake. This is a time when we need a special kind of environment and care so that we can recover balance in our life and begin to heal.

A bardo interrupts the busyness of normal life and shocks us into a resting point, a sudden stillness, like tripping on the sidewalk and breaking your arm. My friend Ida had a positive view of this interruption: "For me, the gift of cancer was that it threw me off the hamster wheel!" This sudden stillness gives us a chance to pause and turn our attention inward, realizing we have with no idea *what* or *who* this mysterious universe of a body is. Being curious, we might discover that our body is more like a bundle of energy than a solid *thing*.

Sudden stillness is a good description of what the word *cancer* did for me. The COVID-19 pandemic had just begun, and I'd already canceled my teaching trips for the year. But now the pause button turned into a full stop. Realizing I had cancer reminded me of the truth that my body would die, and it could be sooner than I think. For the first time in my life, my main occupation was to learn to love and care for my body: "I see you; I feel you. I'm here with you. We're going to be in this together." This was my message to myself at the time, and it's my message to you now as you face whatever your bardo has presented you with.

FROZEN BODY

When asked to validate his enlightenment, the Buddha is said to have proclaimed his truth by touching the ground. "The earth is my witness," he said. Being still, holding steady in our bardo and listening to our body, we can do the same. We're home in this moment on this earth. It's a friend we can learn to trust. Being in a relationship with our body is the first step in our bardo journey, and we do this by training in mindfulness. Mindfulness can be thought of as a moment-to-moment awareness of our body, emotions, and thoughts. Here, mindfulness is introduced as a listening practice, a loving presence that you can offer to yourself. The meditations and contemplations in this book will continue to support you in becoming more mindful.

With loving presence, we can learn to recognize our habits of shutting down and ignoring the energy in our bodies. These mindless habits prevent us from having a living relationship with our bodies. Instead of listening to the ongoing flow of information from our bodies, we identify with frozen concepts and opinions about what our bodies should be. When this happens, our communication system is down. For example, during my cancer journey, I noticed how often I've tried to overrule my body's fatigue with caffeine or sugar. But during chemotherapy, my fragile digestive system made those options impossible, so I had no choice but to finally listen, let go, and rest. I also realized that mindlessness has another negative outcome. When we neglect our own body, we cut ourselves off not only from our own life force but also from the field of relationships that can nourish us as well as from the beauty of the natural world.

Like an earthquake, a bardo has a beginning, a middle, and an end. When the ground stops shaking, we will emerge changed in some way. The shape of our new normal will depend on how well we've been able to embrace this frozen fear so that we can stay awake with loving presence.

Recovering our balance in stillness is the first step in our bardo journey. We're learning to make friends with our body, our center of gravity in a changing world.

Contemplation
STILLNESS IN CHANGE

- Contemplating our own inner wisdom, we can see that truth usually speaks to us in paradox, more like poetry than ordinary logic. Here, the paradox is that being busy and speedy is what keeps our body frozen. When we're in stillness, we discover and accept the energy of change. Is this true for you? If so, say more in your journal.

(continued)

- What judgments, opinions, or concepts block your experience of your body as it is right now?
- How do these ideas relate to fear?
- What do you appreciate most about your body?

Meditation

BODY SCAN

10 MINUTES

A body scan meditation will help us start to feel embodied, at home in our skin, and more receptive to listening to our body.

Begin in a sitting posture and gently sway from side to side a few times. Then gradually come to rest, relaxing into stillness. Feel the weight of gravity holding your body to the earth.

Welcome the movement within stillness, listening to the energy in your body. Close your eyes and imagine that your awareness is a liquid light.

This liquid light slowly makes its way with warmth, clarity, and love through the interior of your body. If you find it difficult to imagine light flowing through the interior of your body, you may do this meditation as if in a shower, with the flow of loving light going over the exterior of your body.

Take your time, relax, and feel this light as liquid love, with affection for the experience of embodiment, soothing the parts of your body that are tense, allowing the natural energy of your body to just be there.

Let the light be like a warm river, flowing around the interior parts of your body that feel frozen and melting whatever feels ready to melt and respectfully allowing the parts that are frozen to be as they are.

Take whatever time you need to fill your body with loving awareness.

Then rest.

2

Allowing Silence

How much better is silence; the coffee cup, the table. How much better to sit by myself like the solitary sea-bird that opens its wings on the stake. Let me sit here forever with bare things, this coffee cup, this knife, this fork, things in themselves, myself being myself.

—Virginia Woolf, *The Waves*

Shortly after my cancer diagnosis, I received a gift of a new Sonos speaker. This was when I discovered that Ziji, our cat, loves music. He looked surprised that our silent apartment could burst into sound. His ears twitched back and forth, looking for the source. Since then, the chatter in our home has subsided into a quieter space. Music has taught us to listen. Like our cat's attention, we alternate from silence to music and back to silence again.

Listening to music helps me listen to silence better, and silence gently awakens feelings of sadness and tenderness that have no words. Silence can be deadening or creative, depending on whether I can make room for this sadness. There were days during the pandemic when silence was like a glass wall, cutting me off from the muffled voices of people on the other side. This is when the sadness froze into depression. But I've also had the experience of sadness blossoming into affection for others during silent group retreats.

Lonely silence attunes us to a subtle communication that flows between us, heart to heart.

When silence opens my heart, the whole environment comes to life, like stars appearing in a night sky. It makes room to amplify all kinds of sounds I don't normally listen to, like onion peels scrunching in my hand on the way to the compost. This is the ordinary magic that a contemplative approach to our bardo journey can offer.

WELCOMING RESTLESSNESS

We've discussed how traditional teachings on the bardo have the urgent request to "Please listen!" We also know how hard that can be, especially when we're in crisis. Even if we have the presence of mind to listen, what is it that we're hearing? What voice can we trust?

We need a certain amount of silence to be able to listen to our body's wisdom. But that wisdom isn't found by pushing away our fear and confusion. The edge of lonely silence can easily tip into depression. No wonder we want to fill that space as quickly as possible with all the familiar distractions that we've used to keep fear at bay. In my family of origin, the mantra of frozen fear was "I'm keeping busy." What was being passed on in our family was this unspoken message: "If I stop and feel this pain, it will overwhelm me, so I'm filling my time to avoid it." I remember as a teenager how this habit of turning away via distraction left me with no path for working with my grief. Remembering that isolation was one reason I began to work with my inner restlessness by training in mindfulness. Restlessness is the hangover from a life lost in activities of all kinds: the deadlines of our schedule, the habit of driving while absorbed in a podcast, the constant checking for the latest text message popping up on our cell phone.

When we're under the spell of mindlessness, trying to keep busy, silence is like dead air on the radio. Restlessness is a lifelong habit that makes solitude, silence, space, and stillness unbearable, like confining a strong young horse in a tiny stall. The solution isn't to squeeze ourselves further. What we need is a large and spacious field to run, leap in the air, and finally come to rest.

When we're restless, we might feel like a squirmy kid who can't wait to get out of the classroom and go play. With loving presence, we can be curious and ask what this inner kid really needs. What are we afraid of? Ironically, we might find is that what this restless kid has always wanted is the very space we've been trying to avoid.

Easing back into silence cools down the fever of mindlessness. We can start simply by interrupting whatever we're doing and pausing for a moment. We'll probably feel a tug-of-war of resistance. We don't want to let go. We want to finish our project, keep watching the movie, or complete our sentences.

My strategy for working with that tug-of-war is to open to silence using beautiful music as a bridge. It brings me home to my body through the portal of my heart. As with the practice of stillness, sometimes I need to move and sway before I gently find my center of gravity. Then I can meet whatever inner wound I've been avoiding, allowing a healing that brings silence back to life.

Contemplation

RESTING

- The contemplative traditions welcome solitude, silence, space, and stillness as the ideal environment for self-reflection. Few of us in our modern life can find the time, money, or place to enter a formal retreat, but it's possible to develop a quiet space within our own heart that we can draw from. How do you experience the transition from restlessness to stillness?

- How do you relate to the sense of sadness?
- What are the differences between aloneness and isolation?
- How does your soundscape practice demonstrate a sense of interdependence with everything around you?

Meditation

SOUNDSCAPES

15 MINUTES

This walking meditation will help us begin to welcome moments of silence as an entry to sounds we normally don't hear in our life and discover new perspectives.

Invite silence by turning off your phone notifications and any other distractions.

Stand still for a moment, focusing on your breathing. Then go for a walk, staying attuned to the soundscape of the environments you pass through. Just listen.

Listen to your inner responses to the sounds you hear. "That motorcycle's too loud." "I wonder what that bird is?" "That dog barking is irritating." "The siren in the distance worries me." When you hear these voices in your mind, just let them go and come back to the soundscape.

When the labeling mind relaxes and listening opens, let the sounds flow in and out of each other. Simply enjoy this without trying to name what you are hearing.

3

A Brave Posture

And I began to recognize a source of power within myself
that comes from the knowledge that while it is most desir-
able not to be afraid, learning to put fear into a perspective
gave me great strength.

—Audre Lorde, *The Cancer Journals*

Before dawn on the day of my surgery, Jerry and I were on our way
to the hospital when suddenly a full moon appeared from behind
a cloud. It reminded me of an instruction that I was given, many
years before I began sitting meditation, for bringing a loving presence to my body.

I was a nervous child with a passionate love for horses. But as
soon as I landed in the saddle, my body would seize up with fear
and I'd grip the reins for dear life. My back would hunch, and my
chest would cave in. It seemed impossible to learn how to relax into
feeling the horse's stride.

One day my teacher told me to imagine a moon in my heart,
like the headlight in front of an old-fashioned train. I would visualize this beam of light coming out from the front of my body and
gradually expanding wider and wider. When I did this, something
deep in my body shifted. It was as though my posture had found
its natural confidence and dignity. The moon opened my heart, my

fear relaxed, and I was able to feel the joy of riding. I could feel the horse and me moving together as one body, her hoofbeats drumming through me.

When I arrived at the hospital for surgery, my body was tense, but I remembered that instruction. I didn't realize how many procedures needed to happen before the operation. It felt like I'd stepped onto a conveyor belt moving me from one specialist to another. My breast was about to get a lot of attention from the medical staff, but my only job was to keep the moonbeam of light open in my heart.

My first stop was in Nuclear Medicine, passing through a door that said Do Not Enter along with the symbol that reminded me of an atom bomb warning. My breast was about to be injected with a radioactive dye. I felt terrified but settled back into the moon in my heart. The needle felt like a beesting, intense but subsiding quickly. I imagined the isotopes in my body like a flow of stars mixing with the moonlight.

Next stop was Radiology. The doctor apologized profusely after several failed attempts to insert two wires into the tumors with ultrasound as a guide. "I'm afraid we'll have to use the mammogram. I'm so sorry," she said. I appreciated that she was a woman and knew from experience what this would feel like. Time to arouse that moonlight. While my breast was being squeezed for what seemed like an eternity, I felt both the pain and the doctor's compassion at the same time. Somehow the absurdity of both of us trying to manage with this medical torture device made me smile. Staying open, even in horrific conditions, can create space for humor.

Finally, I was wheeled into the operating room and greeted by my surgeon with her fuzzy gray hair drawn into a bonnet. She reminded me of a grandmother preparing a warm batch of cookies rather than a skilled doctor hunched over her tray of surgical instruments. I felt safe and ready to let the moonlight lead me into the darkness, with no idea what my new body would be when I woke up. The last thing I remember was the moonlight in my heart dissolving into the brilliant light above my surgeon's head.

MOON IN HEART PRACTICE

Think of the love that liberates us from fear as a full moon appearing during the darkest of nights. That darkness is our denial, our habit of freezing and turning away from the truth of the present moment.

Our body can teach us how to be brave if we know how to attune to the flow of energy within it. We simply straighten our posture, lift up our head and shoulders, and open our chest. My teacher suggested imagining that our heart is connected to a kite, blowing in the wind of the present moment. We feel everything. This is how awake fear opens our confidence.

When we tune in to our heart center, in the middle of our chest, there can be an unexpected relaxation, a sigh of relief. The barriers of frozen fear melt and we restore a relationship with the present moment.

Tuning in to our heart allows us to be nourished by kindness. The qualities of love are fully present as a two-way street. We're grateful to the people who are mothering us, and we feel compassion for our own pain and the pain others are going through. The moon symbolizes this interdependence. Like a loving mother, we can't leave our own confusion or the confusion of others behind.

Courage isn't something we impose on ourselves. It's like a flash of moonlight that arises briefly but illuminates a bigger view. Then the darkness of night sets back in again. The practice is to remind ourselves of this when we feel our chest caving in with fear. Under all circumstances, we can awaken this bravery and love in our heart.

As a child, I sometimes imagined being Joan of Arc, getting on my horse and saying, "I can do this." But now I understand that when my heart is open, when I'm in relationship with the present moment, I can't *not* do this.

Contemplation
YOUR OPEN HEART

- Imagine the tenderness of your heart like a full moon appearing from behind a cloud on a dark night. This moon of loving-kindness gives you the strength and resilience to stay open to fear rather than shutting down. Feel the qualities of an open heart—tenderness, bravery, and a touch of sadness. Write about personal examples of being willing to ride the energy of goodness, to have confidence to open to and face challenges in your day life.
- What does this inner power tell you about the relationship between love and fear?

Meditation
FULL MOON OF THE HEART
10 MINUTES

In this meditation, we attune to the power of our dignity and courage by working with our posture.

Sit still, in silence, with your body in a posture like the Buddha—relaxed but upright. The Buddha's posture is an example of a visual instruction on how to restore our body to its natural wakefulness.

(continued)

magine a moon in your heart. It doesn't matter what size it is; you don't have to hold a visual image, just feel its presence in the heart center of your body.

Notice the effect this has on your posture.

Simply rest in this posture, letting your body adjust itself as it wishes.

Remember to come back to this image and this posture as often as you like during the rest of your day.

4

Breathing

What we call "I" is just a swinging door which moves when we inhale and when we exhale. It just moves; that is all.

—Shunryu Suzuki, *Zen Mind, Beginner's Mind*

When I woke up in the recovery room after surgery, the compression bandages made it feel like my chest was buried under a concrete block. I had to relearn how to breathe while feeling immobilized by this unnatural weight on my body. In the days that followed, I scrolled through my tablet for stories about ordinary people who became heroic in times of crisis.

One example was the rescue of the boys' soccer team who were trapped in a flooded cave in Thailand for over two weeks in 2018. The courage of the rescuers is world famous. But I was also inspired by the team's twenty-five-year-old soccer coach, a former Buddhist monk, Ekapol Chanthawong, who helped the boys deal with panic in the cave by teaching them mindfulness meditation, using the breath to stay present.

In the uncertainty of a bardo, it's easy to feel trapped like the kids in the cave. Imagining them in the dark, without food or water, made the bandages on my chest feel tighter. But the story reminded me to put down my tablet, try to relax, and feel the tender movement of my breath under the compression bandages, like feeling for a pulse to reassure me that I was alive. Practicing mindful breathing is the best way to reverse the panic of claustrophobia.

PANIC AND LOVE

I've suffered from claustrophobia most of my life, often on bridges or in crowded elevators or buses. Once, I had a panic attack while driving through a long tunnel with my young baby in the car seat. I couldn't breathe. My heart was pounding, and my mind was racing with the dread of losing control of the car. But I was a new mother and suddenly remembered I wasn't alone. I had a baby to protect. This realization dissolved the panic so quickly it surprised me. It was as though the mother in me took over and my fear could ride safe and secure in the back seat with my child.

Remembering this, feeling the compression bandages oppressing me like a straitjacket, I reimagined that sensation to be like a baby swaddled to my breast. Turning toward my fear with loving-kindness, I was able to relax and just breathe.

Relating to panic isn't easy. It's not enough to simply imagine the love of a mother. It's more helpful if you can fully embody this reassurance by swaying or rocking from side to side and protecting your mind with a simple melody. When I was in labor, my midwife coached me to sing, "Row, row, row your boat gently down the stream . . ." You might have a little tune like this that you can use to soothe yourself when you feel overcome by fear.

AIR HUNGER

Another panic attack taught me something valuable about the nature of fear in relation to the breath. The panic attack was triggered by a *clank* that echoed down the hallway as the last gate closed, locking me into a maximum-security prison. I was there with my colleague Joe to introduce meditation to a circle of twelve men. As my panic increased, I felt the walls closing in around me, escalating the dread that I'd lose control. Frozen fear was like a demon in the basement of my psyche that could appear at any moment: "Who do you think you are, pretending to be a meditation teacher when you can barely breathe!"

Thank goodness, Joe took over and began our session. My heart was racing as he introduced the meditation: "Let's begin by feeling the rise and fall of our breath in our body." I could barely hear his words. My throat was contracting like a hangman's noose. "Now, let's turn our attention to the out-breath." Joe spoke quietly. "Just *be* the breath. Identify with it. Let's do this all together, whispering the sound *Ahhhhh . . . Ahhhhh . . .* just relax and let the sound dissolve into silence."

His words seemed far away. I started digging my fingernails into my hand to try to keep control. To stay on the roller coaster in my mind, I decided to try counting each breath, in and out. But I couldn't find my breath.

The nature of panic is that it causes you to freeze up, often making you unable to take an in-breath. It's sometimes called "air hunger." In panic, we're trying to catch the in-breath with the same urgency that we must have had at birth when our survival depended on it. A panic attack feels like we're fighting for our life.

When I finally caught my breath, it was a huge relief, a sign that I was out of that box and would make it through. But my heart was racing, and the panic was still in charge.

Slowly, as if coming back to life, I remembered the instruction to identify with the out-breath. Joe was leading another round: "*Ahhhhh . . . Ahhhhh . . . Ahhhhh . . .*" The institutional soundscape of the prison softened with the men's voices, whispered almost as if in prayer.

At last, I was able to do it, to breathe out and let go. At this point, something unusual happened. The panic dissolved into its exact opposite—a stable, peaceful space. It felt like taking off in a plane on a windy day, bouncing around in the turbulence and then suddenly resting in the clear blue sky above the clouds.

I admit that this was only one experience out of possibly dozens or even hundreds of panic attacks I've had. But once you've seen the clear sky on the other side of panic, you don't forget it.

When one of the men asked, "What about the in-breath?" Joe replied, "Your body will do this naturally; just return to the experience of being here now." I smiled, imagining a loving mother at the wheel of a car, turning and saying to me, "Don't worry about trying to survive, you've already done it! Welcome home."

BIRTH AND DEATH

Panic is a preverbal struggle with birth and death that grasps for breath as if for the first time. It's the most abrupt version of fear that we can experience in a bardo. But the key is to flip that struggle around—instead of trying to catch our breath, we can reverse our attention and breathe out, creating space. We don't need to have a panic attack to appreciate the way that the out-breath stabilizes our mind in the present moment. But we do need the gentle voice of loving-kindness to use in conjunction with the out-breath: "Come back, come home, I'm here, you've survived. It's okay."

In some ways, a bardo is a slow, extended version of a panic attack. It's a disruption that disconnects us from a sense of predictability. We don't know what will happen next. So, we can all benefit from learning to relate to this kind of fear. It's not an easy journey.

To anyone who experiences panic attacks or the kinds of abrupt challenges and losses that can and will occur in a bardo, I understand how difficult that can be.

The meditation practice of letting go with the out-breath with a smile is a powerful training in letting go of that struggle and trusting our body. Smiling with the out-breath is subtle, but it brings a feeling of victory, making room for both birth and death, breathing in and out. We let go into the momentary gap, breathing out, and learn to trust that the in-breath will take care of itself. As Joe said, we can trust that our body knows how to do this.

Contemplation
RESPONDING TO FEAR

- The two examples of panic attacks I shared in this chapter resolved in different ways. The first was with love (remembering my baby while feeling panicked in the car), and the second was by opening to space (by focusing on the out-breath). These experiences of tender heart and open mind are central to how we will work with the middle stage of our bardo in part two. What is your own experience of fear erupting without warning?
- Imagining an experience of fear erupting without warning right now, can you bring loving-kindness to that fear in the form of your breath?
- When you experience fear, what happens when you smile, imagining a loving mother taking control of the car and the fearful part of yourself, like a child, tucked away safely in the car seat?

Meditation

LISTENING TO OUR BREATH

10 MINUTES

This practice for using our breath to stay connected to the present moment is the foundation for training in mindfulness.

Rock from side to side, then gradually bring your body to stillness. Feel the moon of kindness in your heart. The back of your body is strong, like a tree rooted into the earth. The front of your body is soft and vulnerable.

Now feel the rise and fall of your breathing, like the tide in an ocean. Sometimes the waves break violently, and at other times they are peaceful.

Allow your breathing to be whatever it is, as a way that your body is communicating the language of your authentic self.

When you breathe out, do it with a little smile at the corners of your mouth.

Let the in-breath happen by itself.

5

Nourishing with Beauty

I learned about the sacred art of self-decoration with the monarch butterflies perched atop my head, lightning bugs as my night jewelry, and emerald-green frogs as bracelets.
—Clarissa Pinkola Estés, *Women Who Run with the Wolves*

"Look up, look closely at that tree. Can you see it? There's a duck! It's sitting there, on that branch." Sure enough, there it was. A duck in a tree. I laughed with delight. Another magic moment in the park with my friend Kim. Her artist eyes always seem to be attuned to a dimension I generally miss.

I had met Kim a few years before my cancer diagnosis. Although she was dying of lung cancer, she taught me that it's possible to be fully alive even in the final months of life. She seemed liberated from linear time, staying awake with fear in the present moment rather than letting it shut her down.

It was fun to walk down a busy street with Kim. She had her own fashion sense; she often wore flannel pajama bottoms with a cartoon design. Her short hair was blond with wave-tips of purple, gently broadcasting that she proudly marched to a different drummer than the rest of us. She was unaffected by the lure of Sale signs in store windows. "Having no future is the freedom of not needing anything more," she said with a wry smile. At least not anything material. When she shopped, it was to find the perfect gift for someone she loved.

Kim taught me that waking up to fear with love was like breaking an addiction to conventional reference points. At the same time, she delighted in her world. Her apartment was a palette of turquoise and beige with walls painted in recurring images of camels delicately stepping through desert sands. Hers was a hidden refuge that few entered. But she invited me in for her last year with the request that I support her in dying.

Kim's immune system may have been compromised, but her mind was resilient. While her lungs were filling up with cancer, her heart became more loving.

NOURISHING WITH BEAUTY

Learning how to nourish ourselves with beauty by coming home to our sense perceptions is the next step in our bardo journey. When we hear that a friend is sick, we send them flowers, music, or food. We have an instinct to express love with sense pleasures.

This is how Kim listened to her body and her world. She taught me how to open my senses. She was like a young child tugging on my sleeve to point out a stream of marching ants on the sidewalk or the progress of a spider making with her web that glistened in the morning sun.

The most precious moments of human experience can be found when we let go of our expectations of how things should be, when we just let the world speak to us in its own language. "If you want to see the duck in the tree, you have to come back to looking the way kids do," Kim explained to me. Relaxing our point of view is like gazing at an optical illusion and suddenly seeing a background figure in the foreground.

Positive Interruptions

Kim and I talked about this way of seeing as an example of what I call "positive interruptions." This is a form of mindfulness practice—welcoming any disruptions in our day as a chance to get off the hamster wheel and listen to what the present moment is telling us.

Even in the darkest times, we can find moments of joy if we experience the delicate fragrance of a wild rose, the song of a robin, or a cool breeze on a hot summer day. Our body responds to beauty because we're nourished by these flashes of wakefulness. Letting go of our expectations, we make room to see something we haven't been able to see before.

A positive interruption is like a mini bardo, and it doesn't always deliver joy. Sometimes it awakens us with fear, like a snake in the grass. But in small doses, that fear can be manageable. When disappointment interrupts our expectations, we can pause and taste the sadness of loss. In everyday life, these flashes of wakefulness occur all the time, but we usually dismiss them as unimportant. The instruction to welcome positive interruptions reverses that habit. We welcome these as glimpses of goodness, nourishment for our soul.

Positive interruptions are like gravity—always there but unnoticed when we're caught up in speed or distractions. By trusting them, we can learn to recognize and welcome any flash of wakefulness that occurs. The practice of mindfulness trains us to interrupt whatever is pulling our attention away from the present moment. This is an unlearning process rather than trying to do something special. But, like breaking any habit, it requires some effort and support.

Contemplation
YOUR POSITIVE INTERRUPTIONS

- How do positive interruptions bring unexpected moments of joy in your daily life? For example, your cat taps you on the shoulder when you're absorbed on your phone.
- What are your ways of practicing the "sacred art of self-decoration?"

Meditation
LOOKING UNTIL YOU SEE

3 MINUTES

This meditation gives us a glimpse of a fresh way of experiencing our sense perceptions, free from the habit of mind that filters them with judgment.

Hold a flower in your hands. Gaze at this flower as if you've never seen one before.

Let the idea of a flower fall away and simply rest your attention on it.

What happens when your idea of the flower dissolves?

Let the color, shape, fragrance, texture of this relationship with the flower speak to you.

At the end of the three minutes, notice how you feel about this flower.

6

Reconnecting to Nature

It is my experience that the world itself has a role to play in our spiritual liberation. Its very pressures, pains, and risks can wake us up—release us from the bonds of ego and guide us home to our vast, true nature.

—Joanna Macy, *World as Lover, World as Self*

Since I was a child, I've gone to the forest for refuge when human logic stops making sense. Lying face down on the soft cedar carpet, I feel comforted, like catching the scent of my mother's perfume. In a forest, my body absorbs a different way of knowing, the wisdom of the natural world. One glance at a new sapling growing out of an ancient stump or the sense of summer turning into fall speaks the language of change beyond the binary of good and bad, birth and death.

After meeting with my oncologist for the first time, I retreated to a nearby park and sat under an oak tree, trying to process what she had told me about the chemotherapy to come. The infusions would start September 1 and end in mid-December. My body, like this tree, was entering a season of loss. Like her leaves, my hair and nails would thin and fall away. Like her, my life force will hunker down to the roots, to my bone marrow. There was no guarantee that my body could weather the storms to come.

GARDEN CONVERSATIONS

My thoughts turned back to Kim and the conversations we had during the year before her passing. Our favorite place to meet was a classical Chinese garden, a hidden treasure in the heart of downtown Vancouver. It's a portal back in time to the Ming dynasty. We entered through a circular-shaped gate and were greeted by groves of bamboo around a reflecting pool. The whole place was designed to evoke an atmosphere of peace and harmony, considered essential for a contemplative scholar in those days. For us, this garden was a soul-space that hosted our conversations about death.

Summer tourists wandered by as we leaned against the ginkgo-wood banister of a little teahouse, watching the orange carp float in and out of sight in the jade-colored water. We began with a little chitchat about the day's activities and news about Kim's friends, family, and health-care team. Then, together, we would gaze ahead into the unknown, as if lifting our eyes from the garden to the sky.

"What do you think it will be like?" she asked one day. I replied, "I have no idea, but the bardo teachings say that, like the natural world, our body is made of the elements of earth, water, fire, and wind. When we die, these elements dissolve and our conscious mind is liberated into space." We paused and fell silent, feeling the presence of the bamboo grove as if it were a circle of ancestors offering us a reassuring blessing.

HEALING RITUALS

As with many Indigenous cultures, Tibetan Buddhism regards the elements as sacred, envisioned as a mandala. Space is in the middle, with earth, water, fire, and wind in the four directions. We think of space as both an ungraspable but ever-present quality like the sky and as our own conscious awareness. Each of the primary elements has both a physical and a spiritual dimension. Altogether, this mandala is a way to envision our human nature in relationship to the world around us. Our body is made of the elements, minerals, water, warmth. They come together with our physical birth and dissolve at death. But when we embrace the flow of change, we discover that there are micro births and deaths happening all the time. By recognizing our relationship to the natural world, we can embrace change as a gift rather than a curse.

"Some changes are not gifts at all. I've accepted that my body is going to die prematurely, but what about the planet, the climate crisis?" Kim asked. "What are we leaving behind for future generations?" Kim felt the distress signals from Mother Nature as no different from the pain, fever, and thirst in her own body. But the scale was overwhelming. There was nothing she could do.

The urgency of climate change is a heavy burden. My Buddhist teachers advise us to pay attention, to stay open and do whatever we can to help. The elements give us a language to communicate with the natural world through art, symbolism, and ritual.

KIM'S PASSING

The following year, moments before Kim's final breath when her hand was getting cooler and changing color, I whispered in her ear, "You're dying now. You're doing beautifully; just touch into your heart, then let go into love." She responded with a little shudder, then relaxed completely. Her passing was so peaceful it was almost unnoticeable.

I sat with her for hours afterward. The space in her room felt dense, like liquid sunlight, an indescribable aura of love, joy, and sorrow.

Contemplation

YOUR NATURE

- When we listen to the elemental messages from our body, we rediscover our interdependence with the natural world around us. Reflect on how your body is a gift from Mother Earth. Imagine, like a forest, there is a kind of health that flows through us regardless of whether we are ill or dying. How do you experience the changing seasons?
- What does it mean to come home to our true nature by loosening the grip of ego?

Meditation

CONNECTING TO NATURE

15 MINUTES

This meditation is a way to connect with the elements and honor Mother Earth. For some, this is the practice of creating a sacred space or shrine in our home.

Arrange symbols of the four elements—a plant or stone (earth), a bowl of water (water), a candle (fire), and a hand fan or flag (air)—in a mandala or medicine wheel formation, in four directions with a symbol for conscious awareness, such as a mirror or a crystal ball, in the middle.

Imagine a similar mandala within your body. The elements of earth as your bones, water as your circulatory system, fire as your metabolism, air as your breath.

Touch your hand to your heart and feel your wisdom and love at the center of your being, invisible, ungraspable, but unchangingly present.

Dedicate your ritual meditation to restoring balance within your body, heart, and mind and extending to all beings and our world.

Rest quietly for a few minutes.

Be creative in developing your personal rituals, using the symbols of the elements to express your heart connection with the natural world during significant events in your life. For example, we might light a candle during a wedding or to honor a loved one who has died. We sometimes release lanterns into the sky to commemorate those who died in Hiroshima and Nagasaki. Sometimes we bathe as a ritual of purification. We human beings recognize that elemental symbols can express a truth beyond words. You can bring this symbolism into everyday life. For example, during the dark months from October to February I like to string lights around my apartment, a habit I learned while living in Alaska.

7

Healing Touch

Both of them remained floating in an empty universe where
the only everyday and eternal reality was love.

—Gabriel García Márquez, *One Hundred Years of Solitude*

I lost my hair two weeks after chemotherapy began. I had all kinds
of preconceived ideas about how this would feel, which, of course,
turned out to have nothing to do with my present-moment reality.
Having shaved my head several times in the past during my years
in retreat as a Buddhist monastic, I tried to wallpaper my anxieties
with the bravado of "been there, done that, so what's the big deal?"

A week earlier, to prepare for the inevitable, I had stepped into
a Magic Cuts salon at our local mall and asked the hairdresser, Fa-
roozan, to cut it as short as possible. "Shall I use the clippers?" she
asked.

"Yes, absolutely!" She clipped the sides but left it a bit longer on
top. Twenty minutes later, I emerged feeling slightly self-conscious
of my transition into gender fluidity, which in some ways I came to
enjoy. It was a different look but still within the realm of normal.
But it was also a powerful no-turning-back reminder.

Then, a day or two later, it started to happen. I began shedding
hair. To manage the situation, I created a ritual of morning and
evening head showers, with the handheld sprayer gently coaxing

hair to rain down to the drain basket in the tub. I would close my eyes until the end, then open to see the furry pile below. The person looking back from the mirror had changed me into a bald and fragile stranger. Not a monastic but more like a very old man with little wisps of hair floating slightly above a tender bald scalp.

NOURISHED BY LOVE

During those early days of chemotherapy, I felt the presence of my dad, even though he had died nearly six years earlier. He had been my first spiritual teacher, full of compassion, the kind of physician who truly wanted to know the details when he asked, "How are you?" He embodied the art of simply showing up, being there with an open heart.

In his final years, my dad was paralyzed by Parkinson's disease. It was unbearably painful to witness his suffering; I felt powerless to help. I had some training from a Taiwanese Buddhist teacher in healing touch, the practice of using your hands as a conduit for love. When I visited my dad, I rested my hands on his bald head, stroking and then holding still, feeling the warmth of love flowing between his head and my hands. His tremors gradually grew still; when I glanced at his face reflected in the window glass, I saw that he'd relaxed into a peaceful sleep.

I took comfort in this memory as I tumbled through my bardo of hair loss, feeling neither like the brave warrior nor the devout monastic. When I stroked my own bald head, I felt my father's hands blessing me with loving, healing acceptance and compassionate presence. I heard the whisper of his voice. I felt like a newborn baby in his arms. Flooded by love and sadness, I felt bathed by the healing exchange of love.

The first blessing we give a newborn is to bathe that new being with love. Years ago, my daughter died during birth. Overwhelmed by grief, holding her in my arms, I felt like my body and hers melted together. The only mothering I could offer my baby was to bathe her in the milk, tears, and blood that flowed from my body to hers. Bathing in love is the first blessing we give to welcome new life into the world and the last one we offer to say goodbye.

RECEIVING BLESSINGS

Reflecting on the truth that each one of us was born and will die can soften our hearts. Imagine blessing ourselves and one another with love in the entrances and departures of everyday life. For many of us, it's easier to give than to receive. But when we're in a bardo, we need help. It's time to let other people know what we're going through, to let them reach out to us and to receive their kindness. Feelings of gratitude and love are powerful reminders that the heart's capacity to open is unlimited.

We human beings are hardwired for relationship, not isolation. Resilience comes from taking down our fences, learning to love ourselves, and reconnecting with the power of openheartedness instead of reacting defensively. We see this in the wake of natural disasters—people and communities coming together to help one another. When we bathe our hearts with love, we understand that a flow of kindness benefits giver and receiver equally.

Contemplation
SELF-BLESSING

- What does healing touch mean to you?
- Reflect on the ritual of self-blessing as the flow of love in and out and through your life. How is love both gently welcoming and letting go?

- How do you find this balance?
- Write about the ways you are nourished by unexpected flashes of tenderness, warmth, kindness, or sadness in response to images or people that touch you.

Meditation

RAIN OF BLESSINGS

TIME DEPENDS ON PERSONAL PREFERENCE
FOR LENGTH OF SHOWER

This meditation attunes us to the way that the brain can heal trauma with gentle sensations on our skin, especially in downward strokes over the head, face, and arms. We apply this by transforming a shower into a healing ritual.

Take your time to enjoy a warm shower. Feel free to sway or sing while receiving the warm sensations of touch on your body.

Imagine that you are receiving a healing rain of blessings on the top of your head, transmitting unconditional love.

Feel that self-blessing flowing over your face, your shoulders, your whole your body.

Imagine this warm, healing water washing through you, inside and out, restoring your whole being to a feeling of goodness, innocence, welcoming.

Make the wish that all beings who are suffering could be touched by this warm, healing rain of blessings.

Rest.

8

Meeting Pain with Love

Becoming intimate with pain is the key to changing at the core of our being—staying open to everything we experience, letting the sharpness of difficult times pierce us to the heart, letting these times open us, humble us, and make us wiser and more brave. Let difficulty transform you. And it will. In my experience, we just need help in learning how not to run away.

—Pema Chödrön, *Practicing Peace in Times of War*

Intense physical pain is a cruel form of mindfulness, narrowing our attention with a laser focus on the interior landscape of our body. It penetrates the self-image we carry about what our body should or shouldn't be and, like a crying infant, demands our full attention on what is.

I had a taste of this kind of pain during the second half of chemotherapy, after my oncologist switched to a new drug. When she told me what it would be like, she paused for a moment, then said, "On days three and four you may feel like you've been hit by a truck."

"Fatigue?" I asked.

"No . . . *pain*. All over your body," she said.

As predicted, the third day after each infusion, the pain began as a tingling sensation in my feet and then expanded upward, as if every nerve in my body was on fire. I watched my mind start to panic: "What's going on? How much worse will it get?" At first, my mind and body were going in two different directions, but as the pain intensified there was nowhere else for my mind to go. There wasn't even room for panic anymore. Finally, there was no choice but to surrender to the pain.

I curled into a fetal position on the bed. There was nothing I could do, nowhere to go, no one to call for help. My body was crying out in a language I didn't understand. My mind dropped to a preverbal level to hear what my body was trying to say. A feeling of motherlove took over as I embraced my body, rocking gently side to side, and sang lullabies to try to soothe the distress.

More recently I've learned that these mother instincts of swaying, whispering, and swaddling have deep, ancient roots for embracing the inevitable physical or emotional sufferings we go through as human beings. My experience was that by relaxing into the pain with present-moment awareness, I could feel its movement, like the turning of a kaleidoscope, through my body. It wasn't solid, and occasionally there were gaps, positive interruptions, small oases of peace.

I'm not advocating that this approach be the only one when you're in pain. Physical pain is the body's way of calling for help. Please don't hesitate to contact your doctor when you're in pain, and taking medication ahead of the curve is always recommended. In my case, the pain was caused by the chemotherapy rather than the cancer, so it wasn't possible to treat it in the usual way. Mindfulness can always be added as a support rather than a substitute for medical interventions.

Contemplation

PAIN AWAKENING HEART

- Wr te about a personal experience of letting pain awaken your heart. What did you learn?
- Re ating to the physical pain in our body can show us how to listen to all the other forms of pain in our life. It can soften the barriers that seem to divide us and awaken compassion for our shared humanity. Has this been true for you in the past? If not, is it something you might be open to in the future?

Meditation

PROTECTING A FRIGHTENED ANIMAL

10 MINUTES

There are three kinds of physical pain: the frozen trauma in our body from the past; the anticipatory pain, bracing for the future; and the pain we're experiencing right now in the present moment.

Envision your body as a gentle animal that you want to protect.

Embrace and rock your body as you would soothe the frightened animal.

Imagine letting go of the frozen pain from the past, as if it's being washed away.

Imagine letting go of the anticipated fear of pain in the future, as if it's a balloon being carried away in the wind.

Feturn to the pain of the present moment and comfort your body with love.

Focus on these words: *I'm here, I feel you, we can do this together.*

The truth of impermanence is a gift when we're in pain. Just stay in the flow of the present moment and change will come.

Let the pain be a bridge to connect with others by making the wish that we all be free of suffering. For an example, reflect on these words: *I'm not the only one suffering like this. May I and all beings be free of suffering and the causes of suffering.*

9

Heartbreak

As anyone who has received or dispensed psychotherapy knows, it's a profession whose mainspring is love.

—Diane Ackerman, *A Natural History of Love*

For years my body was trying to tell me something, but I wasn't listening. One day I asked my doctor if she knew what caused my cancer. "No one knows for sure, but you had a normal mammogram eighteen months ago, so this grew very quickly," she explained. "Your lab tests show that for the last two years your white blood cell count plunged below normal. Your immune system was down. Were you under any stress?"

That was the moment when I realized that my personal bardo began before I knew I had cancer. I nodded to her but couldn't begin to explain how I'd just lived through two of the most difficult years of my life.

RESPONDING TO BAD NEWS

It began one afternoon when I was sitting in a garage in a small, unfamiliar town, waiting for my car to be repaired after it had broken down on the highway. My phone pinged a text message from Jerry that would turn my life upside down. Our granddaughter, Maya, had just died of an accidental drug overdose. The words on the phone turned blurry. I felt lightheaded and dizzy but, at the same time, my chest felt like it weighed a thousand pounds. The concrete floor seemed to sway under the plastic chair I was sitting on. My face started burning. Heartbreak is so literal; it felt like my ribs had cracked open, releasing a flood of sensations through my body. My mind was spinning, trying to make sense of this new information. But my thoughts kept unraveling. My story had no place to go, like finding myself at the edge of a cliff or the slippery slope of a melting glacier.

At that moment it felt as though every emotion I had in my life, when released from their stories, came home to this overwhelming sadness. I got up and stumbled out of the garage into the parking lot, looking for a safe place to pull myself together. I felt like I was walking in slow motion, turning from the dusty main street down a lane lined with backyards and clotheslines and little bursts of wildflowers coming up through the gravel. "There will be time later to make sense of this," I told myself. "Right now, all you need is just to find enough space to absorb the impact of this bad news, feel it in your body, hold it tenderly in your heart."

Safe Shelter

When bad news comes as a shock, our body-mind-heart reverberates with a spontaneous instinct for self-compassion. We can't help but feel our humanness, our vulnerability. But we might bypass that open wound if we don't have a safe place to take shelter and a way to listen to our emotions.

Maya's death was the first of three losses that happened one after another in the weeks that followed. What I didn't realize at the time was that the overwhelming fatigue in my body was more than grief. It was a symptom of the cancer growing out of sight in my breast. Cancer fatigue is hard to describe. It hits suddenly and completely, sometimes in the middle of a conversation or while driving—when I barely had time to park before falling asleep.

The fatigue in my body and grief in my heart tipped me into a dark and confused state of mind. I decided that I needed to talk to a counselor. This would be the first time I would be at the receiving end of the listening space I'd been offering to others for decades, and it was harder than I expected to make this switch. I didn't know Ellen, the counselor I'd chosen, except that she had an interest in spirituality and mindfulness. She was also a musician, which intrigued me. In our first session, none of that mattered. Her body language, the expression on her face, welcomed me with unconditional acceptance. This is what I needed.

Cradle of Kindness

Ellen offered gentle encouragement as I struggled to describe my situation. She gave me space for the stories of the past to find a soft landing in the present. This is the kind of listening space we need when we're hit with emotional storms in our bardo. The bad news might be a diagnosis, a sudden betrayal, or a tragic loss. Our life has fallen apart, and the future is open. We need a compassionate friend who can hear our bad news without freezing it into blame or toxic opinions. To do this, we need someone to handle our vulnerability very tenderly.

Heartbreak cracked open my pride and led me to ask for help, to receive as well as give, to be grateful as well as generous. In a crisis, the flow of kindness is what truly keeps us alive. It's like a restorative aquifer of water that lies buried underneath the politics that divide us. My Buddhist teacher used the image of a cradle of kindness as a shelter for our fearful mind. When our heart is broken open, we need support from someone who can offer unconditional friendliness, a listening space that encourages us to stay awake instead of freezing. This is a relationship that allows a fluid dialogue for our stories, insights, and worries to be spoken without solidifying them into opinions or judgments.

There have been difficult times in my life when I couldn't afford professional counseling, and I know there are readers who may be in that situation now. Sometimes all we need is one friend who can listen. Going for a walk together is a good way to bring healing energy to the body as well as the heart. You also might find grief support groups through hospice or other local organizations. Heart-friends protect our vulnerability so that we can stay awake with fear, as well as with joy and sadness and the range of tender-hearted emotions in between.

Contemplation
JUST LIKE ME

- Heartbreak is a great equalizer. It's a human emotion all people share. Recognizing this vulnerability in others brings an openness, beyond judgment, that allows us to see them as having the same tender heart as ourselves. Consider this shared humanity. What is it like to stop judging yourself and others and simply rest in the feeling of others being "just like me," feeling your shared sensitivity?
- This flowing together is the energy of love, putting ourselves in another person's shoes: "I see you; I feel you; I'm here with you." Comment on this in your journal.

Meditation

A FLOW OF KINDNESS

10 MINUTES

In this meditation, we return to the practice of loving-kindness, holding the pain in our heart with tenderness.

Feel the pain of a broken heart with compassion. Compassion is the wish to relieve all forms of suffering, our own and others.

Include your own grief as a way of connecting with the suffering of others, beginning with any beloved person or animal that touches your heart.

Feel this heartbreak ripple outward, like waves in a pond, to feel the pain others feel, including friends, strangers, and even people we think of as enemies.

Pause and breathe.

How does this feel in your body right now?

If you like, place one or both hands on your heart.

Meet Frozen Fear with Compassionate Wisdom

When the external wound and the internal wound begin to meet and to communicate, then we begin to realize that our whole being is made out of one complete sore spot altogether, which is called "bodhisattva fever." That vulnerability is compassion. We really have no way to defend ourselves anymore at all.

—Chögyam Trungpa, *Training the Mind and Cultivating Loving-Kindness*

W hile it cannot be measured by time, there is a certain midpoint in our bardo journey when we feel disoriented. This is where we begin in part two. It's like being in a boat in the middle of the ocean: the shore has disappeared, our destination is nowhere in sight, and the structures of our daily routine have dissolved. For me, the effects of the COVID-19 pandemic isolation and the toxicity of chemotherapy felt like a long, dark Alaskan winter. I was sleepless at night, fatigued during the day, and foggy-minded most of the time. My eyes were too dry to read, so I passed the time listening to music and audiobooks. The music soothed my heart, and the stories offered an escape into fantasy worlds. In the background of my mind was a dimly lit awareness, a trace of curiosity that remained after decades of meditation training. It was as if a part of me was observing the whole experience: "Ah, so this is what a bardo is like!" It felt as though my body, mind, and heart had melted together.

A FLOATING WORLD

Floating through life may sound appealing, but the danger of having no ground is that we can get lost in our mind's imagination. The midpoint of a bardo is when we start believing our mind's projections to be real. Thoughts of the past rise as enemies. Our memories taunt us with self-accusations about the mistakes we've made or simmering resentments about the harm others have caused us. We long to reconnect with lost loves and unresolved relationships. We toss and turn in emotional storms triggered by these untethered story lines. What we need is the shelter of a loving presence that can comfort and reassure us with self-compassion and forgiveness. Instead, our habit is to seek solid ground by clinging to unexamined belief systems, the masks of frozen fear. The bardo teachings offer guidance about how to avoid these pitfalls when our path gets treacherous.

STAYING WITH BODY

In the early stage of our bardo journey, we learned how important it is to listen to our body as a way of staying awake. The ground has shifted; we need to pay attention. Like the weather and the seasons, our body has always been showing us the truth of impermanence, but when we deny that reality, we silence this message, believing things should stay the same. Now, when our emotional storms hit, it's time to let go of our preconceived ideas and take a closer look. Letting go of the past is essential if we want to change our relationship to fear. We must look at the truth of our interdependence rather than our habit of hiding behind barriers, and at how our life has always been nourished by the flow of human kindness. When things fall apart, it's time to trust our vulnerability. By opening our heart, we can receive care and love from others—friends and strangers alike.

The problem with the middle phase of our bardo is that this is the point when wakefulness turns back into denial and our old habits kick back in. These emotional reactions make our situation worse. I've known some people to quit chemotherapy at this point, convinced they can find alternative treatments. I can understand how they felt, but sadly I've also learned how many of them died prematurely along the way. In the emotional storms at the midpoint of our bardo, we might feel like we're losing our mind.

FROZEN FEAR: INNOCENT MISUNDERSTANDINGS

If you recall, while awake fear protects us from harm, frozen fear is the opposite. Frozen fear is the impulse to close our eyes and hold tight when we feel threatened. The price we pay for this innocent misunderstanding about how to protect ourselves is we're unable to listen, hear, or fully pay attention. So, the practice for this stage of our bardo is to meet ourselves at this edge, at the point where we shut down. We can sympathize with how painful this fear is. Our ground has fallen away and our emotions are running wild. We can't rely on the past to predict the future, and the present moment can feel confusing and unfamiliar. This dark night of the soul is a spiritual crisis, a time to hold our mind and emotions tenderly. But how do we do this?

The first stage of our path is nourishing the roots of mindfulness and loving-kindness with the practices of listening to our body. Now, to work with frozen fear, we need to listen to our mind and heart. For this we'll turn to the teachings on *bodhicitta*. *Bodhicitta* is a Sanskrit word for an awakened heart, also described as a mother's love for all beings. *Bodhi* means "awake"; and *citta* means both "mind" and "heart." When Buddhists talk about mind, we point to our chest, not our head. The heart and mind are one, but this heart-mind has two qualities: a clear awareness and a tender responsiveness. This compassionate wisdom is the flowering of our inborn capacity to appreciate our life beyond any sense of personal territory.

MEETING EMOTIONAL STORMS

The instructions on bodhicitta are a reliable guide because they originated from a crisis that was similar in some ways to our own. The Buddha left the comfort of palace life after being shocked by the suffering of illness, old age, and death. I imagine him hearing the words "You are going to die" with the same kind of awake fear as I did. He then entered his own bardo journey with the intention to discover for himself if freedom from fear was humanly possible. Sitting under a tree in meditation, he made room to observe the play of his thoughts and emotions, curious about the root causes of our suffering.

We're told that in the last hours before his enlightenment, the Buddha was attacked by all kinds of emotional storms—projections of his mind that appeared as terrifying enemies or seductive lovers. But the power of his compassion made him immune to their attacks, transforming the rain of weapons coming toward him into flowers. After his awakening, the Buddha remained silent, knowing that what he had seen about the true nature of our human heart was impossible to put into words. But when his friends pleaded with him for help, he began to teach.

The cause of our suffering, he said, is clinging to the wrong idea about who we are. We're in the habit of turning away from the tender energy of our own goodness. This is frozen fear—ignoring what is true. Our false identity is like putting on a suit of armor and forgetting what our own skin feels like. The path of bodhicitta, awakening our heart, is a process of uncovering our vulnerability, stepping out and experiencing our life nakedly with compassion and courage. As we proceed on this path, we will apply these teachings to penetrate the dualistic barrier that imagines ourselves being cut off from others.

In our bardo, we experience the unavoidable suffering of change. It may take the form of loss, sickness, or aging. With loving presence, we can meet these challenges with comfort and encouragement. A bardo can also be an identity crisis, shaking up our idea of who we are. If we can apply the teachings on bodhicitta, awakening the true nature of our mind and heart one step at a time, our bardo challenges can show us how to transform the weapons of frozen fear into flowers of awakening.

10

Being Curious

It's very rare to be in a state where there's nothing in, where you have no attachment to any idea or concept about yourself. In that state you've immediately raised the mind of compassion, because if nothing is in, everything is in, and you are now free to experience yourself as the world.

—Jeff Bridges and Bernie Glassman,
The Dude and the Zen Master

One day, halfway through my chemotherapy treatment, my friend Joanna called. "How are you doing?" she asked.

I tried to summon a description. In most ways I was feeling okay, putting one foot in front of another. At the same time, the drugs were affecting my brain and I was experiencing a kind of memory loss and confusion that was unfamiliar. "I sometimes feel I'm lost in a fog," I told her.

Then Joanna asked, "How do you know you're lost?" Her simple question ignited my curiosity. Somewhere behind the fog there was clarity. Instead of reacting to my confusion with fear, I could trust my own basic sanity. If there was enough insight to recognize that I'm lost, that insight could be a beacon I could rely on to find my way home.

Being curious about our own confusion is the first step in making friends with our mind. Our basic sanity is a natural truth detector, the best survival tool we have.

It takes a lot of mental energy to disable common sense, but when we freeze our heart with fear, we also freeze our curiosity. A frozen mind doesn't have the flexibility to let go and truth-test information. Without discerning fact from fiction, we can be lured by false certainties, conspiracies, and misinformation. Our intelligence turns in on itself and tricks us with mental stories that aren't rooted in reality.

MAKING FRIENDS WITH CONFUSION

Frozen fear closes our eyes to the truth of our present-moment experience. This is only a habit of mind, a reaction that began when we had no other way to defend ourselves. The point isn't to judge this as bad but to bring warmth and understanding, to see clearly how this defense mechanism is no longer helpful. Turning toward our own confusion with curiosity is like affectionately inviting a frightened animal to emerge from their hiding place. We see the bigger picture—that the habit of not paying attention only increases our imagined fears. We recognize this as a dangerous pattern, especially when we're in a bardo.

A WELCOMING SPACE

"How do you know you are lost?" Joanna's question reminded me of the approach we take in contemplative psychotherapy. We trust that our basic sanity can wake us up from our own confusion if we're curious about how we know what we know. There's a Buddhist teaching story that illustrates this. A young child is in her mother's lap at a party. The child is enthralled with the sights, sounds, colors, and activity around her, but suddenly panic sets in. She doesn't see her mother anywhere. She feels lost and terrified. Her mother then turns her around, so they are face to face again. The child relaxes into her loving embrace. Frozen fear melts instantly when we turn around and recognize the true nature of our heart.

In my counseling practice, the welcoming space I offered was an external version of the listening space I created for myself with sitting meditation. This is where I found confidence in the healing power of basic sanity. Contemplative psychotherapy gently invites us to turn around with curiosity and meet our own mind, face to face. When it's backlit with trust in our own awareness, we can meet our frozen fear with love and learn to recognize our own wisdom when it arises. Heartfelt attention offers stability and encourages us to disentangle our stories and let our emotions sort themselves out.

The tender wisdom of bodhicitta enables us to listen to our thoughts and emotions without getting pushed around by them. But we can easily lose our way if we don't have a method for discerning what is true and what isn't. The practice of sitting meditation retrains our mind to turn toward our basic sanity, our inborn truth detector, so that we can meet the challenges of our bardo with an open, flexible, and curious mind.

MAKING FRIENDS WITH OUR MIND

When the Buddha declared that the cause of our suffering was clinging to our self-centered stories, he wasn't advising that we go in the opposite direction and be completely detached from our experience. The key point is that we don't have to identify with them. We can learn to unglue our fixation. Our thoughts, stories, and emotions can come and go, but if we don't identify with them, they won't cause harm. *Identifying* is labeling these mental events as "me." Like getting absorbed in a movie, fixated attention these mental events, making them seem more real than they are.

Making friends with our own mind is no different from getting to know someone else. When we're interested in learning more about another person, we listen carefully. Our mind is open, but our attention isn't stable for long. At some point, we're distracted by our thoughts. The same is true in meditation. Listening to our own mind, we discover how easily we get carried away by trains of thought, even if they're upsetting. It's like being addicted to the news on our screens. Even painful stories can capture our attention. By contrast, returning our attention to the present moment is boring—"nothing happening."

The Buddhist meditation technique for training our mind to rest is called *shamatha*, which means "abiding peacefully." We turn toward our basic sanity as a listening environment, the space in which we can observe our thoughts and emotions come and go. Over time, training our mind in meditation can stabilize our attention so that we can be present in that space a bit longer. But like any relationship, it takes time and patience. We're simply listening, but not in the usual way when we're caught in the grip of our thoughts and emotions. Instead, we're training to notice the gaps in our thoughts and let go, coming back to the open space of our awareness as if meeting a new friend.

Being Curious about Thoughts

My meditation students often want to know more about how to use this technique to relate to our thoughts. I find the image of a train of thoughts helpful. In meditation we repeatedly find ourselves riding that train. But with a flash of basic sanity, we notice we have an alternative. We can recognize where this train is heading, choose to get off, and let the train go by. Over time, we might realize that we can simply watch the train. We might see through the gaps between each car to the landscape on the other side.

Our trains of thought are full of gaps. The only thing holding them together is our fixated attention. That fixation makes them seem real. This is the clinging that the Buddha identified as the cause of suffering. Meditation teaches our mind to be curious about these gaps when we let go of the stories that can carry us away.

By relaxing the grip on our thoughts, we discover that our basic sanity is a bigger awareness, a listening space that's already there. It's like that dim light in the fog I recognized when Joanna asked me how I knew I was lost.

With meditation, we're strengthening our ability to pay attention. When thoughts, emotions, or any form of distraction carry our mind away, we gently interrupt them and bring our attention back to the present moment, using our breath. This is how we learn to listen to our own heart and mind.

Finding a Balance

In meditation, our attitude is not to get rid of thoughts but rather to just let them be what they are, a natural process of the mind. But at the same time, we're breaking the habit of always letting them capture our attention. It takes a while to find the balance between not being too tight and trying to suppress them or too loose and just going along with them. The balance comes from not identifying with the ups and downs of our thinking process as who we are.

The point is to relax, let go, and be curious. Curiosity depends on trusting the experience of *not knowing*. This is how we learn something new about someone else, and the same is true about ourselves.

INSIGHT DAWNS

At some point, as the thoughts in our mind settle down, we might get more curious about this open space of our own awareness. For instance, we might begin to wonder, "Who is it that interrupts my thoughts? Am I the speaker of my thoughts or am I the listener? What's this big mind beyond my thoughts? How did I know I'm thinking. How do I know I was daydreaming?"

The curiosity that inspires these questions is described in the Buddhist tradition as our first glimpse of the Great Mother, Prajnaparamita. She is like the loving mother holding the child in her lap. She is the space of our mind that gives birth to enlightenment. Sometimes we use the terms *basic sanity* or *basic goodness*. But the word *bodhicitta* encompasses both the openness of our natural awareness and the tender texture of that space. It's both an open mind and a loving heart.

Contemplation

AWARENESS OF THOUGHTS

- Like a beam of light shining through the fog, bodhicitta is a way of knowing, an awareness. This listening space of the mind is often compared to the sky, where thought clouds come and go. It's always present, always listening, but it's ungraspable, so our habit is to bypass it most of the time. We take it for granted, like the air we breathe. This is also the tender space that can grow into unconditional love. Think of an example of a time when you changed your mind and suddenly saw a situation with fresh eyes. How did this affect your emotional response to that situation?

· What do this change of mind and fresh way of seeing mean to you?

Meditation

PEACEFULLY ABIDING

10 MINUTES

Please note that an emotional storm isn't the easiest time to rest peacefully. So, if we're in the thick of it, it's best to begin with the practices in part one first, listening to our body with movement and stillness, turning to nature, or finding comfort from a friend.

Create a space in your home that feels uplifted. As you become more familiar with the practice, you can gradually increase the time in ten-minute increments up to an hour.

Being with a short body scan, relaxing all the joints and muscles of your body from head to toe.

Bring your body into an upright posture. If you like, you can imagine a moon in your heart, which uplifts your head and shoulders in a gentle but dignified way. It helps to relax your throat by opening your mouth a little, as if saying "*Ah.*" But you can choose to keep your lips closed if you like.

Turn your attention to feeling your breath moving in and out of your body. This will be the object of your meditation, your breath.

(*continued*)

You might feel it coming and going like a swinging door, in and out. But gradually rest your attention, identifying with the out-breath rather than with your thoughts.

Generally, as a beginner's practice, regard anything that distracts your attention from the breath as "thinking." It could be a sense perception or an emotion, but just label it in your mind as a thought.

Each out-breath—"*Ahhhhh*"—brings your attention home to the present moment. It's as though in your inner conversations you're switching from speaker to listener. This simple shift takes patience and discipline, but it's a life-changing skill.

Continue to do this repeatedly as the meditation technique until your timer rings.

Please note that if you find it too difficult to use the breath as an object of meditation, you can use something visual, like a flower, a photo, or a sacred object such as a statue of the Buddha. The breath is helpful because it's always with you. But to train your mind to be present, it's possible to use any object that brings your attention back to nowness.

11

Awakening Our Heart

Kinship—not serving the other but being one with the other. Jesus was not a "man for others," he was one with them. There is a world of difference in that. I suppose I never felt this kinship more keenly in my own life than when I was first diagnosed with leukemia.

—Gregory Boyle, *Tattoos on the Heart*

I was sitting in the waiting room at the cancer clinic one morning, socially distanced from the other patients, wondering what kind of suffering they were going through. I wanted to hold their hands, hear their stories, reassure them that they were not alone. The pandemic had ended support groups and human-to-human conversations that are so necessary when people are going through the same kind of crisis. The only option was to join an online group.

Women around the world who were similarly isolated posted messages to one another. Because triple-negative breast cancer strikes mostly younger women, many posts were from mothers with little kids. One morning I read a post from Anita, a young single mother who was terrified of dying, leaving her two children as orphans. I looked out the window and remembered what it felt like to be a single mother, afraid that death would come too soon, before my child was on his feet. Now I was in the best situation possible to have cancer—cared for by a loving partner and my adult son thriving on his own. I tried to imagine Anita managing chemotherapy while caring for young children.

I made the wish "If one of us should die soon, let it be me." It felt half-hearted at first, as if I didn't really mean it. After all, I wanted to survive. My brain-mind knew it wasn't possible to truly take on Anita's situation and replace it with mine. But I was grateful to have my normal thoughts interrupted by my heart-mind, a flash of bodhicitta.

OPENING TO OTHERS

Flashes of open heart show us a bigger view, beyond the barriers of frozen fear. The instructions for cultivating bodhicitta apply to any situation in which we find ourselves. We're training our mind to see the world through the eyes of a Buddha. For example, when we're in pain, we think of others who are in the same boat, and then we expand the size of that boat to include all beings.

When I made the wish to change places with Anita, it was because, for an instant, I loved her as if she were my own child. I would exchange my life for hers. This made no rational sense, given that I had never met her in person. Like the experience of meeting the begging child in Nepal, this gave me a taste of what openness feels like. We have moments like this all the time, but without knowing what to do with them, we bypass them and return to the habit of separation. The bodhicitta teachings tell us to regard them as precious, to recognize these heart-flashes of openness as our own authentic nature and to cultivate them by training our mind and heart to go along with them rather than shutting them down.

Bodhicitta is a love that never dies because it's not located in the brain. Attuning to this nature of mind softens our fear of pain, aging, change, and death because it opens us to a bigger way of knowing. Learning to listen and feel this tender heart is how we transform the suffering of our bardo into resilience.

EXCHANGING SELF FOR OTHER

One way to cultivate bodhicitta is to arouse gratitude for the support we've received from others. I reflect on the way that my therapist, Ellen, was able to create a welcoming space for me. She was delighted when I was open, patient when I froze, and encouraging when I couldn't feel my tenderness at all. She forgave my feelings of regret and resentment when I felt angry with the people in my life who'd harmed me. She leaned forward with compassion when I turned that anger inward, criticizing myself. Her heart seemed to have limitless space to accommodate my grief when it felt like I was drowning in it.

Ellen created a compassionate container for me by providing a safe outlet for my emotions. When we're in pain, we're vulnerable. It's like having an open wound in our heart. It helps to have a trusted friend or counselor who knows how to listen, so that we can process our fears without shutting down.

Considering how much we've been given, we can then learn to be that friend to ourselves by creating a listening space in meditation that's strong enough to hold and transform the emotional pain we bring to it.

PATH OF AWAKENING

Tonglen, exchanging self for others, is a Buddhist practice for awakening our heart that dissolves the barriers that isolate us from the people and experiences we're afraid of. It reverses the habit of frozen fear by letting go of our own comfort and switching attention to the suffering of another.

In tonglen we begin by invoking gratitude by recognizing that our well-being has always depended on the generosity of others. Buddhists consider that in countless former lifetimes, everyone we meet today has at one time or another been our mother.

Once this openhearted relationship is established, it's painful to helplessly witness another person's suffering. In tonglen we can imagine offering this person all kinds of practical things—a warm home, food, a cure for their illness. But the ultimate gift is to wish that they can rest peacefully in the spacious goodness of their own heart.

Contemplation

TONGLEN

- Tonglen is a profound practice and a lifelong training, but a more familiar example of exchanging ourselves for others happens in our conversations. When we listen, as Ellen did, we're putting our own interests aside and welcoming another person's suffering into a space that can transform it with love. Reflect on what happens when you listen to another person's pain with complete attention. Can you identify what this feels like in your body, your heart, your mind?
- What is the point when you meet your edge and you're unable to listen? How does that feel?
- Reflect on all the various ways you listen from the heart in everyday life, paying attention with any of your senses.

Meditation

EXCHANGING SELF FOR OTHER

10 MINUTES

Breath by breath, tonglen is using our imagination to reverse the habit of frozen fear by activating our compassion. When we feel powerless to help, the practice of tonglen gives us a way to stay present. Being able to stay present even for only one moment longer can show us the true power of our human heart.

Begin by resting for five minutes.

Bring to mind the image of a person or animal whose suffering touches your heart.

Make the wish to relieve them of their suffering in any way that comes to mind. Perhaps you imagine giving food to a starving child or shelter to someone who is unhoused. You might imagine comforting someone who is dying alone.

Turn that wish into a practice: Imagine that you are breathing that person's or animal's suffering into the open, tender space of your own awakened heart. Then as you breathe out, imagine you are giving relief to them.

This exchange of the in- and out-breath is like imagining your whole being to be like an air purifier in a smoky room. You're offering a suffering person or animal the clean, healthy air of bodhicitta from your heart and breathing in the polluted air of suffering that you normally want to reject. But you don't consider that this

(*continued*)

in-breath will be toxic to you; you're not sacrificing yourself in a neurotic way. Instead, you imagine the suffering dissipating into the limitless space of your heart, becoming completely pure.

By the end of your tonglen practice, imagine that the person or animal you've been thinking of is relieved of their suffering, then expand this to visualize that all beings are relieved of suffering, beyond all limits. Keep this tonglen practice relatively brief, for five minutes, and conclude with five more minutes of resting meditation.

12

Working with Regret

Once you face your fear, nothing is ever as hard as you think.

—Olivia Newton-John

I found the courage to go through chemotherapy because I trusted that my doctor was monitoring how much poison my body could handle. I depended on her because the killer in my body was a painless lump. What made me feel sick was the poison my doctor gave me as medicine. In the turbulence of my mid-bardo emotional upheavals, this reminded me of my teacher's instruction: "Transform the poison of negative mind into the medicine of compassion." This teaching became my anchor. I repeated those words slowly, thinking, "Where is my negative mind? I'm not feeling it right now." I paused to scan my body. Nothing there. I felt numb, like a shadow of myself. Then I started writing in my journal.

There, stories started to emerge about my resentments, memories of people who'd hurt me in the past. These icebergs were hidden, and I was reluctant to admit they were there. But they were as deadly to my soul as the cancer in my breast was to my body. Here was my chance to discover how poison could be medicine.

STEPPING OVER THE LINE

Through journaling I remembered an incident that happened a few years ago. I was having dinner with friends when the conversation turned to politics. I felt myself starting to escalate. Looking back, I realize how much I had been depersonalizing the others at the table, as if lecturing to cardboard cutouts. I gave them no opportunity to respond; I wasn't curious about the view from their side of the barrier. I kept talking, building steam, and ended up accusing a friend, someone I loved, of being heartless because of her political beliefs. "You just want to make people disappear into prisons. You don't see them as human beings!" I exclaimed. I knew right away that I'd stepped over the line and hurt her but couldn't take it back. It was a painful lesson. I had just done the very thing I accused her of doing—disappearing her. She's one of the most compassionate people I know.

I was awake all that night thinking about what I'd said. She was so vulnerable. I had trapped her in my logic without giving her a chance to say, "No, this isn't okay. I need to be heard too." I was ashamed of the whole episode. In my mind I begged her to forgive me, but I knew it was too late to undo the harm my words had caused.

My intention to stop causing harm was intensified by this wish that I could go back and repair these relationships. At that moment I understood the importance of forgiveness, mercy, and love, not only for my imagined enemies but also for my frozen self. We all suffer from the same confusion.

CONFUSED EMOTIONS

From a Buddhist perspective, a closed mind is like a neglected body, chronically unhealthy. Just as an unhealthy body has symptoms, like a fever, to warn us to pay attention, a neglected mind suffers from emotional fevers. When we imagine ourselves to be cut off, we lash out with aggression, jealousy, or craving.

This is one of the problems with frozen fear. It doesn't show its face directly because it's masked by these defensive emotional reactions. If we get curious about painful emotions, we can see that they don't help at all. In fact, they always cause harm—to ourselves and our relationships. Buddhists refer to confused emotions as *kleshas*. Unlike the tenderhearted responses of bodhicitta, kleshas originate from our mental stories, not from our present-moment reality.

Kleshas may seem like relatively painless feelings at first, but they're destructive. Like cancer cells, they spread quickly, poisoning our mind and our relationships. Kleshas are fueled by stories that aren't true. If we're angry, we're convinced we have the right to punish. If we're addicted to someone or something, we're sure we deserve that person or thing and will do anything to get what we want. The logic of the emotion gives us permission to act itself out.

In the traditional teachings for the middle stage of a bardo, a compassionate friend speaks to us as if we're hallucinating: "Don't be confused; your mind is playing tricks on you." In the bardos of everyday life, one version of this compassionate friend is the feeling of regret.

WORKING WITH REGRET

Regret is a painful medicine that's hard to swallow. But like chemotherapy, it's better than the alternative. If we're willing to listen to regret, it will be a reminder the next time we're blinded by frozen fear, so that we can interrupt our mental stories before we act them out.

Regret is like waking up with a terrible hangover. We're disgusted with ourselves, wanting to forget what we said or did, wishing the whole memory would just disappear. But if we can bring insight and loving-kindness to our feelings of regret, we can use those painful experiences to clarify our intention to love. So, try to welcome the pain of regret as a teacher rather than shutting it down with shame. Ask yourself what kind of relationships you want to have with others. Are we truly interested in listening to other people or are we shutting them out? Regret softens us so that we really hear others instead of trapping them into roles in our personal drama. If we can hold steady in the quivering space of regret, feeling the pain of our barriers, we can melt those barriers with compassion.

Regret also leads to resolutions, such as "I promise I'll never do that again." It gives us a more panoramic view, truth-testing our story lines by looking at where they're leading. Do they increase love and kindness or increase suffering? Taking this bigger view is how regret can unmask our blind spots, melt frozen fear, and re-connect us with the true power of our heart. This is the medicine that heals our suffering rather than making it worse.

Contemplation
ACKNOWLEDGING REGRET

- Regret shows us our frozen fear, which is a suffering that no one inflicts on themselves or others intentionally. Bringing understanding and compassion to the pain of this barrier, we can melt that fear back into its original innocence. Give yourself space to reflect before writing. What kind of emotional environment do you need to meet regret with compassion and self-forgiveness?
- What practical steps can you take to give this compassionate environment to yourself?

Meditation

BEING YOUR OWN COMPASSIONATE LISTENER

20 MINUTES

In this meditation, we use the pain of regret as medicine to heal our suffering and the suffering of others. We do this by seeing clearly that the causes of suffering are the barriers between us.

By listening, we learn the language of the heart and become familiar with our frozen emotions. If we get curious about them, without acting them out or suppressing them, we can discover that the true nature or the energy of those emotions arises from our basic sanity, bodhicitta.

Allow ten minutes to begin with self-reflection. Place your hands on your heart if you wish. Feel the goodness of your body, as if it is holding you in a loving embrace.

Rest quietly, reflecting on an example from your life when a frozen barrier triggered you to say or do something you regret. Feel the pain of that frozen fear as a universal cause of suffering.

Welcome the clarity of mind that sees this suffering of the barriers between us.

Come back to your heart and feel the sadness that comes with losing connection to others and to your true self. Let that sadness proclaim the vow "Never again!" This is the extraordinary medicine that can reactivate your healthy emotional immune system if you promise not to forget what you've learned.

(continued)

Tasting the vulnerable feeling of regret is touching the pain of frozen fear. Don't beat yourself up for it. Welcome this insight.

For five minutes, practice tonglen (pages 92–94) for yourself with this intention. If you like, you can make gestures with your hands to support the practice.

Extending your arms with the out-breath, touch the poison: open your heart to the suffering of this frozen barrier, your own as well as the experience all beings have when we shut down our hearts.

Embracing your heart with the in-breath, turn the poison into medicine by bringing it home with the resolution to liberate all beings, including yourself, from frozen fear.

Do this practice three times.

Rest for five minutes, feeling your tenderness, sadness, and resolution to go forward on this path.

13

Four Pillars

Nothing like stars to show us our little arguments are meaningless.

—Glendy Vanderah, *Where the Forest Meets the Stars*

It's a blessing to be able to use poison as medicine, even if the side effects are painful. In the previous chapter, we saw how the feeling of regret can heal our relationships when it shows us how we mindlessly harm others. The promise we make to refrain from doing this again is like a New Year's resolution: easy to say, hard to keep. The teachings on bodhicitta offer a path to reverse our ego defenses so that we can stay present with vulnerability when we meet challenging circumstances.

Imagine that you are hiking on an unfamiliar trail and suddenly your path is blocked by a raging river. You're stuck on one side of the river but determined to cross over. The river symbolizes our negative states of mind—the kleshas referred to in the bardo teachings as "the lower realms." The determination is our resolution to overcome those patterns. Bodhicitta, it is said, is like a bridge, an easy way to cross the river without getting swept away by these endless cycles of suffering.

In the next few chapters, we will unpack this symbolic image of a bridge and apply it to our bardo journey. We begin by reframing our regretful resolutions into positive terms, making it easier to identify with a vision of goodness. This is the fourfold aspiration called "the four limitless ones."

THE FOUR LIMITLESS ONES

When seeking a bridge over suffering, especially the pain of addictive clinging, we cultivate the first aspiration, loving-kindness for all: *May all beings be happy and have the causes of happiness.*

To cross over the river, especially the realms of hatred, we cultivate the second compassionate wish—the desire to liberate all beings from suffering: *May we be free of suffering and the causes of suffering.*

To cross the bridge over the lower realms of jealousy, we aspire to joyfully celebrate the successes of others and be forever liberated from doubts in our basic goodness: *May we not be separated from the great joy, beyond suffering.*

To avoid the whirlpools of self-importance, we train to recognize the limitless tenderness of our shared humanity: *May we dwell in the great equanimity, free from passion, aggression, and prejudice.*

This is a profound practice that guided me during my cancer journey. But I found that this bridge of bodhicitta needed additional support with a practice I call "the four pillars."

This is something I learned during a previous bardo journey, the nine years of retreat at Pema Chödrön's monastery, Gampo Abbey.

THE FOUR PILLARS

As with all bardos, my retreat at Gampo Abbey began with an awakening to the shock of impermanence. The inspiration to leap into the unknown dawned while Jerry and I were grieving the stillbirth of our daughter. The future we'd carved out for our baby was now an empty space, so we decided to take a break from our careers to focus on spirituality. As soon as our son left for college, we flew out of our empty nest, heading for Cape Breton, Nova Scotia.

Gampo Abbey's retreat center is located near the main monastery on a cliff overlooking the Gulf of St. Lawrence. It's surrounded on three sides by a fence with a gate, above which are the words, in Tibetan, *Sopa Chöling*, a "place to practice patience." Our teacher, Thrangu Rinpoche, chuckled when he told us that a group meditation retreat would be the best way to train in bodhicitta: "The irritation from other people will help you cultivate these qualities."

The retreat began with a ritual called "the gate ceremony," when the participants say their goodbyes to friends and family and enter one by one. This ceremony concludes by closing the gate, symbolizing a boundary that would protect our contemplative community from the distractions of the outside world.

The first time I walked through the gate I was terrified. Here at last was the ideal situation for awakening my heart. In the long months that followed, I started each day by reciting the four verses that express our deepest human longings: the wish to be happy, to be free of suffering, to experience joy and, finally, to remain in equanimity beyond the ups and downs of our reactive emotions. But I soon realized how difficult this practice is. Reflecting on these noble aspirations during a quiet morning meditation gave me a glimpse of bodhicitta, but the interactions with my fellow retreatants often illuminated how I fell short. As the retreat progressed, it felt as though the gap between these heartfelt wishes and the gritty challenges of everyday life grew rather than shrunk. I realized how much support we need to turn toward, meet, unmask, and melt the habits of frozen fear that divide us from one another and from our own hearts.

I reflected on the example of bodhicitta as a universal bridge allowing all beings to cross over the realms of suffering. My version of this bridge urgently needed stronger foundations. So, I expanded my visualization to include four pillars, the supports I was relying on in my retreat: friends who offered a culture of kindness, turning toward my own pain with self-compassion, relying on the insight of basic sanity, and, above all, meeting my frozen edges with patience.

In my work as a contemplative therapist and Buddhist teacher, I've met people just like me, who want to be happy, to be free of suffering, and who often feel brokenhearted, unable to help the ones they love. I hear in them the same intention that I had when I walked through the gate at Sopa Chöling. These teachings on bodhicitta, along with the pillars that support it, can be life-changing during difficult times. During my cancer bardo, I turned to these practices again, and I've decided to share them with the hope that they will benefit you. I will briefly introduce them here and explain them further in the upcoming chapters.

1. Kindness Circle

When things fall apart in our lives, we need the support of people who share the intention to keep our hearts open. This special friendship is the first pillar, similar to the Buddhist concept of *sangha*, or "community." I encourage my students and clients to consider meeting with a few like-minded friends in small groups called "kindness circles." In my mindful communication work, I refer to these as "green zones." Friends who hold the intention to be openhearted embody the first bodhicitta aspiration—the wish that all beings be happy, at peace, and in harmony. We can't find happiness in isolation. Companions on our path teach us that the roots of happiness are found by caring for one another with loving-kindness. In our bardo journey, this kind of intentional circle of friends is the first pillar that can stabilize us when we meet emotional storms. We'll go into more detail about this in the next chapter. Readers who are interested in the "green zone" structure can learn more about this in my book *The Five Keys to Mindful Communication*.

2. Self-Compassion

The second pillar is self-compassion, the process of making a relationship with our own pain with love and acceptance. This aligns with the second bodhicitta aspiration—the wish that all beings could experience relief from suffering and uproot the causes of suffering. Sometimes it seems easier to care for others while neglecting our own pain. But authentic compassion has to begin with ourselves. In the groundlessness of a bardo, we have a chance to see our situation with fresh eyes. Self-compassion opens a relationship to the parts of ourselves we've been afraid to meet. To bring that suffering to our heart, we come face to face with the bully voices of our self-criticism, the masks of frozen fear. Once we meet and understand our suffering, how it's rooted in the habit of turning our back on our own pain, we can bear witness to the suffering of others as no different from our own.

3. Insight

The bardo is dangerous because it's easy to become disoriented when our reference points have fallen apart and we're in a state of emotional upheaval. The third pillar for the bridge of bodhicitta is insight—the clarity of mind that sees through our self-deceptions. With open eyes and heart, we unmask the bully voices of our core fears and recognize our own goodness. Insight supports the third aspiration—the wish that we, along with everyone else, could experience this goodness, free of self-doubt. Insight shows us a bigger picture, that it's possible to be free of the unnecessary suffering created by our barriers.

4. Patience

Above all, in a bardo crisis, we need to protect the relationships we depend on. The fourth pillar reminds us how to do this. At critical moments we can train to stay open rather than to shut down. This is the practice of patience, communicating from the heart. It's a pillar that supports the fourth aspiration—that all beings may dwell in great equanimity free from passion, aggression, and ignorance. This great equanimity is the true nature of our heart, the tenderness that nourishes our relationships.

It takes a long time to melt the barriers that divide us. Every conversation is an opportunity to do this. It's humbling to realize how easily thoughts can turn into words, and words can grease the wheels for action. This pillar brings our vast intention down to earth in the nitty-gritty moments when we have a choice to either open or close. Meeting those edgy moments with patience protects us when we're about to get into trouble. If we chose to open, we can discover that equanimity is the shared experience of our vulnerable human heart.

THE PILLARS AS A HOLDING ENVIRONMENT

The middle stage of a bardo is an emotional period. We need a way to sort out what our emotions are truly saying underneath our frozen patterns. Thankfully the Buddha left us with a map that we can follow and a bridge for crossing over the roaring river of our negative habits. The practice of the four limitless ones, supported by these pillars of protection, show us how to meet fear with insight, compassion, and wisdom. In the next four chapters we will apply these teachings to our bardo journey. Step by step, crossing the bridge of bodhicitta, we can turn toward, meet, unmask, and finally melt our frozen fear patterns.

Contemplation

FOUR PILLARS

- Kindness circle: It's difficult to walk this path alone. A kindness circle can be created with as few as one or two friends who share the intention to turn toward fear with curiosity and love. What is your experience of a listening environment that feels safe and openhearted? Who in your life shares your intention to make a relationship with fear rather than bypassing and freezing it?

- Self-compassion: What is the difference between self-compassion and compassion for others? Which one do you find more challenging? How does self-compassion support you in meeting your own suffering—being willing to touch it and feel the pain of your barriers?

- Insight: Reflect on any examples that come to mind of suddenly having an insight into your fear-based patterns that you didn't see before. Where does this insight come from? Insight on a healing path can show us our underlying goodness and healthiness. Is this true?

- Patience: Patience supports us to hold steady at the tipping point when we feel hurt by the barriers between us. Reflect on how patience protects your relationships, especially when you're feeling hurt or vulnerable. What's your personal experience of holding steady in that vulnerability, patiently speaking or listening to someone with an open heart? What's your personal experience of the opposite: reacting to that sensitivity with the push-pull habit of dismissing someone without caring or trying to pull them into your territory?

Meditation

THE FOUR LIMITLESS ONES

15 MINUTES

This is a contemplative meditation based on the first two aspirations of bodhicitta. We should allow equal amounts of time to first read the words out loud or silently and then pause and listen to our heart.

Allow ten minutes for the first part of this practice. Relax in a comfortable physical space where you won't be interrupted. Create a welcoming environment for emotional energy, listening to your body using any of the practices from part one, such as rocking side to side and then resting in stillness. It might feel supportive to place a hand on your heart.

Read the following words: *May I and all beings be happy and know the causes of happiness.*

What does happiness feel like? Visualize someone or a pet that you love and feel the wish for them to be happy.

Expand that wish to as many beings as you can.

Listen, feel, and welcome this quality of loving-kindness.

Read the following words: *May we be free of suffering and the causes of suffering.* What is the suffering we can be free of? How does it feel to make this wish?

Visualize someone or a pet that you love and feel the wish for them to be free of suffering.

Expand that wish to as many beings as you can. Feel and welcome this compassionate quality of the human heart.

Allow five minutes to rest and listen to your heart. Let go of thoughts and words and simply rest, listening to your inner truth. Feel the emotional energy moving through your body. When thoughts arise again, gently interrupt them and come back to the present moment using your breath. In that space, allow something fresh and new to arise.

Close by renewing your intention to practice loving-kindness and compassion, using your own words.

14

Kindness Circle

A great deal of chaos in the world occurs because people don't appreciate themselves. Having never developed sympathy or gentleness toward themselves, they cannot experience harmony or peace within themselves, and therefore, what they project to others is also inharmonious and confused.

—Chögyam Trungpa, *Shambhala:*
The Sacred Path of the Warrior

A great concern for those of us in a bardo is isolation. We can feel isolated even in a crowd if we're surrounded by people who either ignore or overreact to our situation. The first pillar of protection is to find a few supportive friends who share our intention to turn toward fear with loving-kindness. These relationships and conversations create an environment that supports us to recognize that the roots of happiness can be found in our interdependence with one another. These roots are nourished when our hearts are open, and they freeze when we turn away and cling to opinions and judgments.

Connection protects us from the eroding effect of a fear-based society that denies the reality of sickness, aging, and death. When mishaps occur in our life, when we become ill or realize we may have a terminal illness, these supportive friends are the companions who help us redefine what it means to be fully alive up to our last breath.

In our families, we want our children and grandchildren to experience peace, and it's painful to see younger generations being bullied in school, afraid of the future and climate change, and feeling alienated. We want to nourish them with love, but we don't always know how to help them. These times of social disruption have plunged us into a collective bardo.

The first aspiration of bodhicitta—the wish that all beings be happy—brings us home to a simple truth: we all have a shared longing for happiness and peace even though we don't always know how to find it. When we look more closely, we can discover that happiness isn't something we can hang on to, like a room full of our favorite things. Happiness is a process of engagement, a flow of love and kindness that depends on relationships. This can be as simple as pausing to say hello and pat someone's dog in the park. All beings, human and nonhuman alike, are nourished by these roots of happiness.

To bridge the gulf that divides us, we need a pillar to protect openhearted relationships, one conversation at a time. This is why it's important to find companions on the path who share your intention to meet fear and suffering with love.

LAS VIEJAS

In February 2020, just before the world locked down in response to the global pandemic, I gathered with thirteen women in Pátzcuaro, a Mexican mountain village, with the intention to apply the principles of bodhicitta to help our world. To do this, we invoked the power of *grandmother wisdom*, which will be discussed more in chapter 16. We weren't all biological grand-mothers, but we were elders in our spiritual communities. In our retreat, we drew from rituals and meditations on the feminine principle in our Tibetan Buddhist traditions so that we could find a path forward during difficult times. The feminine principle is described as a mother lineage—the source of tenderness, compassion, and communication in our world. This is also the wisdom that liberates us from fear. Deities such as Tara are symbolic of that lineage, but each one of us, regardless of gender, can access this feminine principle in our own heart.

We had traveled to this retreat from north and south—from Alaska, British Columbia, Ontario, Maine, California, and Texas. We had no idea that the pandemic was around the corner, and I wasn't yet aware that a deadly cancer was growing in my breast. We didn't know what would unfold in our seven days together, but we trusted that as older women, we could tap into a collective wisdom. We needed clarity to be of help to the younger generations in our families and communities. We needed to see the crises they face through the eyes of a wise grandmother, our way of transmitting the mother lineage. To do this, we spent most of the week in small groups of two or three, opening our hearts to one another in these kindness circles. I thought of these as stem cells for an enlightened society.

In the twenty-first century, we're dominated by a fear-based materialistic culture that's afraid to look at death and dismisses older people as irrelevant. For my friends and me, this isn't the legacy we want to pass on to our children, nor is this the culture we identify with. As bodhisattva warriors, we're crossing a bridge to a different vision of society, a compassionate culture that treasures the wisdom of our ancestral lineages and *las viejas*, the elder women, as sources of knowledge.

REALMS OF SUFFERING

We gathered in Mexico as a pillar of friendship to revitalize this vision. One conversation at a time, we lifted our spirits and reflected on our lifetime experiences, harvesting what we'd learned in order to nourish our younger students and friends. Our vow as heart warriors is to do whatever we can to liberate all beings from fear. By awakening bodhicitta, we're building a bridge to cross over the realms of suffering. Like starving villages, the emotional environments of samsara are cut off from the roots that nourish us. Instead, they feed on opinions and divisiveness. The frozen barriers between us block empathy, and we end up mocking the vulnerability that is so vital to our emotional survival. We neglect our childlike longing for connection and become like hungry ghosts heading for the snack food aisle. The pain of rejection makes us desperate to belong at any price. We join the bully club, where we bypass our original feelings of being hurt by hurting others.

Like a pandemic, the suffering of samsara is contagious and spreads through our conversations. For instance,

> When mindlessness rules and we don't listen to each other with warmth and curiosity, this fear-based culture takes root in our homes and communities. Discouraging conversations become normal. No one would deliberately say, "Let's get together for lunch and gossip about our mutual friends so that we'll end up feeling more mistrustful and unhappy." But when we don't pause and look at what we're doing, this is what can happen.[3]

As a family therapist, I sometimes imagined having a bird's-eye view of a neighborhood, wondering what social environments were being cultivated in each house below. Were some children being welcomed into a culture of love, laughter, and creativity? Were others next door hiding from violence or made invisible by a culture of speed, competition, or paranoia? The same might be true for a workplace, a school, or a circle of friends. You can discover what realm you are in by the stories people share with each other—the conversations that certain social environments allow and the ones that are silenced. For example, some of these cultural filter systems create an environment of paranoia and mistrust while others might increase competitiveness.

NOURISHING WITH WISDOM AND INTENTION-SETTING

In our retreat, we contemplated how these realms of suffering arise from frozen fear. Like water, the true nature of our emotions is fluid and nourishing. The path to liberation from samsara is melting the fear that divides us. This is possible when we envision the alternative to samsara: a culture of kindness. We acknowledged that the place to begin is with our personal relationships. Like a grandmother soothing a young child, loving-kindness gives us confidence to turn toward fear with love. This is the path of gentle warriorship that leads us out of the realms of suffering. We gathered in Mexico to restore this kind of supportive community, to feel our own dignity, and to celebrate.

As the retreat leader, I offered a structure that would enable us to feel our hearts so that we could deeply listen to ourselves and one another. Our mornings were silent, with meditation and walks in the garden. Later in the day, we broke into our small kindness circles to share stories of our lives. In the evenings, we sat in front of the big fireplace, feeling our sisterhood with laughter and occasional tears. The schedule was like the line drawings in a coloring book; as the retreat progressed, the pages overflowed with color, laughter, vigor, wisdom, and love.

The last day of our retreat concluded with a delicious feast and singing and dancing around the fire into the night. Our joy was like a basket to collect the wisdom we'd gathered in our time together. We didn't forget our intention for being there. Before we said goodbye to make the journey home, not knowing the pandemic would make this the last time we'd physically be together, we made a dedication:

May we dedicate our lives to restoring peace and harmony to our homes, to our communities, and to the whole world.

May we bring the warmth of compassion to the frozen fear in our hearts when we're trapped in reactive patterns and do the same for others.

May this tender space of the heart ease the suffering of all beings.

May the blessings of all our spiritual ancestors support us on this path.

MOMENTS OF COMMUNITY

I realize how unusual it is to live in a spiritual community as I did at Gampo Abbey. I also appreciate that it isn't easy to enter a retreat, like the one we had in Mexico. But we can create a small kindness circle to engage in meaningful conversations with trusted friends. Some people do this in a book club, being able to talk and listen to one another, going in-depth on topics they value. Others form small groups of three to five people who agree to meet regularly and to follow guidelines that serve like the pillars of protection.

Contemplation

INTENTION FROM INSPIRATION

- Recall one example of a positive message you received from your grandmother or another elder in your life. Who are the ancestors that inspire your wisdom and compassion?
- Who are the people who inspire you most, who you want to gather and celebrate with?
- What is your personal dedication to helping the world, the next generations? Refer back to the dedication on the previous page to see which line resonates most with you.

Meditation

EXTENDING AND EMBRACING

10 MINUTES

In this meditation, we're using the embrace of a loving grandmother as a compassion practice. We can apply this to the sadness we feel when reading the news or dealing with painful conflicts in our family, workplace, or circle of friends.

Begin by reflecting on the first limitless one: *May I and all beings enjoy happiness and the causes of happiness.*

Contemplate the support you find from friends who are loving. Think about how the conversations around you either support or suppress your awakened heart. What kind of realm are you in today?

Sit quietly for a few minutes.

Imagine seeing the realms of suffering from a larger perspective, like an eagle looking down at the landscape below. These could be images from the news, such as the suffering of political disruption, war zones, or people and animals starving in drought-stricken countries.

On the out-breath, extend your arms and hands, connect with the suffering of these beings who are trapped in helpless situations.

On the in-breath, bring your hands to your heart with the wish these beings could be free.

Adapt this contemplative meditation in any way you like, to stay in relationship to the suffering of frozen fear and the wish to liberate all beings into a culture of kindness.

15

Self-Compassion

This life review is not an exercise in autobiography but rather an inquiry into meaning. We review our lives to make sense of them.

—Merrill Collett, *At Home with Dying*

The second pillar of protection is self-compassion. While there are many ways we can experience compassion for our own suffering, in this chapter we will focus on opening to emotional energy that we're in the habit of suppressing. This relates to the second limitless one: *May I and all beings be free of suffering and the causes of suffering.* Some of us are afraid to express certain emotions, based on our personality style or past experiences. If we've witnessed violence or been harmed by aggression, we might be afraid of anger. If we've been punished for our vulnerability, we might be afraid to experience our tears. We might be afraid of our sexuality or of being overwhelmed by longing.

One approach to meeting the parts of ourselves we've been suppressing is to do a life review. In this chapter I'll share my experience of discovering self-compassion by reading my old journals. Seeing the roots of suffering within ourselves is the starting point for being able to see how all beings suffer from the same misunderstandings.

LETTERS FROM THE PAST

My doctor didn't come right out and say the words "It's time to get your affairs in order," a coded message that means death is around the corner. Nonetheless, having cancer during the pandemic lockdown, I had time on my hands to do so. I took a fresh look at the small apartment I share with my husband. He loves Zen-like simplicity and is always trying to create space. In contrast, I'm like a hoarder, holding on to decades of journals, notebooks, and a library of books. Death doesn't always come with a warning. Did I really want anyone to have to deal with all this stuff after I'm gone?

I found a shredding company that would show up at our door and dispose of hundreds of pounds of notebooks and documents. With no more excuses to delay, I reluctantly pulled from under the bed a dusty plastic box full of my old spiral-bound journals. These were the stories of my life, going back nearly fifty years. Was I ready to toss these into the shredding bag? Why did I hang on to them for so long? I must have secretly hoped that someday I'd look back and make sense of the tumultuous path of my life.

I glanced through the pages in the earliest journal, words pouring out in colorful ink with the backhand cursive from my high school years, with drawings of horses in the margins. These were like letters from the past to the future, a teenage girl telling of her despair about the unraveling of her parents' marriage. I remembered the dead-end feeling my life had at such a young age. It was a bardo of loss and shame for the overwhelming sadness I couldn't shake off. Most of the other entries were written late at night, smoking cigarettes, when I was feeling trapped and alone. It occurred to me that I couldn't just mindlessly throw them away without honoring the SOS message they were sending. At some level, my younger self was hoping that someday her suffering would finally be heard, that her stories would finally make sense.

The later journals included love poems—the passionate yearnings, the thrill of romance, the roller coaster of longing, disappointment, and the final crushing heartbreaks. Reading and remembering, I whispered to that young woman, "You're not unlovable. You are brave, vulnerable. Don't punish yourself for your broken heart."

COMPOST SUFFERING

The emotional residue from the Mexico retreat gave me the courage to take a closer look at the past harms I had caused others when I was flailing around in my emotional storms. I was overcome with shame and regret and wanted more than anything to reach out to those people in the past to tell them they were innocent, to beg forgiveness. It was too late; they were lost in time. We had met and parted, and the trajectories of our lives had gone in different directions.

I remember something my teacher said about how to look back on the dark times in our past: "It's good to remember those times so you can be of help to others. You know what it feels like. Compost your suffering and use it to nourish the garden rather than throwing it away." In other words, we can always recycle our negative energy and make it positive.

I was able to put my journals into the shredding bag but with a promise to continue to listen tenderly to the voice of my younger self and to see her reflected in everyone I meet.

When I read my old journals, sometimes it felt so painful I wanted to stop. But opening to those memories with self-compassion kept my heart open. When I remember my son's vulnerability, losing his baby sister on his first day of high school, I want to protect all the boys who cry easily and are bullied for their sensitivity. Remembering my own adolescent depression, I want to reach out to young girls to comfort their sadness.

Merciful wisdom composts our suffering so that it softens us, nourishing a culture of kindness and vulnerability. We can celebrate our life story as what it feels like to simply be human beings—complex, tender, and brave.

SPIRITUAL AUTOBIOGRAPHY

Self-compassion comes from revisiting our stories with loving-kindness and allowing them to speak their truth. We might have suffered during dark times without a friend, but it's never too late to reunite with the lost child that we were. It's time to be that mother to ourselves, to listen to our suffering with loving presence.

For each of us, our life story is a spiritual journey. There are dark nights, hidden times when we are out of sight, suffering depression or failure when we feel betrayed or grief-stricken. These are the bardos that change our life in some way. Reauthoring our life story is a chance to revisit our past—to touch, feel, and taste the texture of those experiences and disentangle from the story lines that bound us there. We gain resilience and flexibility when we can edit our self-image and welcome the person we are today.

COMPASSIONATE LIFE REVIEW

Compassionate life review is a way of meeting our memories in the listening space of a loving mother, holding them gently while letting go of the story lines that bound us in an identity that we've outgrown. It's possible to edit our self-image and welcome the person we are today.

Panoramic vision is timeless. Rather than thinking of our past bardos as failures or dark shadows, we can revisit these periods of disruption and see them as sources of valuable information. It's never too late to melt frozen fear, letting go of judgments and criticisms and the destructive emotions they trigger. There is some truth to the adage that time heals our wounds. When we look back at a painful memory—for example, at a time when we felt betrayed in a relationship—we have a chance to see how the larger story played out. Taking a moment to pause and melt our held resentments is how we can release that pain. We might think, "I see now that that person wasn't right for me. I took the betrayal personally then, but now I understand that this rejection wasn't proof that I was unlovable."

Forgiving ourselves and having mercy for others is a healing process some people spontaneously go through when preparing to die. Others bring the stories of their lives into therapy, where their traumas can be held and healed in a compassionate listening environment. But with mindfulness and intentionality, you can begin this healing process for yourself right now.

SELF-COMPASSION

The second pillar, self-compassion, supports our wish to relieve suffering and the causes of suffering. When we soften our frozen fear, we experience the energy of our heart as fluid. All our emotions are relational. They are shaped by the stories we're told and the ones we tell ourselves. Self-compassion arises from gently receiving our frozen memories with warmth and acceptance.

Life review is a healing process of extending the love from our present self to the pain and confusion of our younger self. Now it's time to listen to our stories and rewrite our biography. We've survived many bardos in our lifetime, but few of them were met with the love and listening space that transforms our suffering.

Listen to the stories of your life with love and respect. How do you frame them? When you think of your life, is it like a frozen photo album or do you focus on your successes, as in a résumé? Do you have a box of old love letters or diaries whispering secrets from the past? How would a compassionate listener rewrite your stories?

LIFE REVIEW EXERCISE

Here is a simple life review exercise that you can build upon as you wish: In your journal, draw a horizontal line on each page for specific time periods. (For instance, you could choose five-, ten-, or twelve-year cycles.) Along each line, draw short vertical lines for each year. Using colored pencils if you like, use symbols or words to indicate the events that happened in those years. When you get to a bardo period, highlight it.

Below each horizontal line, make note of the impact these events had on your sense of identity.

Another option is to draw your timeline as if it were a road map, with symbols or the landscape along the road indicating the events and bardos.

To fill in the emotional picture, play songs that remind you of each of these periods in your life. Give yourself enough time to feel, dance, or sway. Then release that memory into the present moment with a sense of self-blessing.

Contemplation
COMPOSTING YOUR FEAR

- Can you relate to the idea of composting fear and pain from the bardos of your past into nourishing growth?
- What does this teaching bring up for you?
- In looking back on your life, what were the emotional environments that either supported or suppressed your soul's yearning to be heard? Take as much time as you need to pause and listen to your younger self, offering love, appreciation, and compassion for the journey you've gone through.

Meditation

WALKING MEDITATION

20 MINUTES

For this meditation, we use gentle movement while contemplating the image of a lotus, a Buddhist symbol for the flowering of our wisdom from the slime and muck of our confusion.

Begin by repeating the words of your bodhicitta aspiration: *May I and all beings be free of suffering and the causes of suffering.*

It is said that when the baby Buddha walked his first seven steps, lotuses sprung from the ground. Sit for five minutes and contemplate the way that a lotus is born out of sight, deep in the muddy base of a pond. Like your body, it is rooted in the earth. Like your life's journey, the flowering of compassion and insight arises from the darkness of our suffering.

Stand and feel the weight of gravity holding your body. Allow your body to find its dignified posture, with your feet rooted to the earth and the crown of your head reaching for the sky.

Take seven steps, walking slowly, with your gaze down in front of you, just feeling each step as if it were your very first step on earth.

Pause and feel your connection to the earth. Then continue to walk mindfully for ten minutes. When you are done, return to your meditation seat and relax for five minutes. Reflect on how the flowering of your life has been the result of bringing a compassionate understanding to your dark times.

As a post-meditation practice, try walking a little more slowly than your normal pace when you are going about your daily activity. Every step is a gift, a present-moment experience that disappears into the past. Enjoy your life!

16

Insight

I think I'm in rather honest company in asserting that there
is an authentic self that's got nothing to do with your life history. You can lose contact with it, but you can never destroy
it, and it's always been there.

—Gabor Maté, "The Myth of Normal: Trauma, Illness, and
Healing in a Toxic Culture," *Insights at the Edge Live*

During chemotherapy I started watching television shows on my
tablet. For fifty-five evenings in a row, I was absorbed in a Korean
soap opera. I imagined myself in a small farming village, feeling a
relationship with each of the characters: the nostalgic old women,
the grifter ex-husband, the silent, misunderstood grandfather.
When the story came to a sad ending in the last episode, I was in
tears. It opened the wound of my father's death, but the grief wasn't
mine alone. It felt universally human. Storytelling is a powerful way
to heal and inspire courage.

After the series ended, I wanted to reconnect somehow with
the show. I found YouTube interviews with the actors who created
these characters. Unmasking them as ordinary people was a bit
disappointing since it broke the spell that held me in the drama.
But it was also liberating. Off the set and out of their costumes,
these people had their own lives, as we all do. But at the same time,

the raw emotional energy their characters had evoked—the feelings of love and loss, anger, and resolution—was our shared human experience.

I felt sad, remembering the twenty years of heartfelt dramas that unfolded in my therapy office. Emotional healing is an unmasking process. The outer story we present can be of a hero who turns into a villain. Or it might be the other way around. Listening with an open heart, we can hear the inner story, the human beings trying to make their way through the ups and downs of their lives. Hearing the story *behind* the story reveals the characters in our dramas for who they really are. That includes the main character: ourselves.

THE STORY BEHIND THE STORY

The third aspiration of an awakened heart is this: *May we not be separated from the great happiness devoid of suffering.* To me, this great happiness isn't some future goal but rather our authentic nature, unmasked from the false narratives we cling to. The pillar that protects this intention is the insight that sees the story behind the story, the truth of our basic goodness. This is the wisdom that sees through our frozen barriers and the core fears that trigger us to shut down. With loving eyes, we see that it's possible to stay connected to goodness, to never be separated from these roots of happiness.

This insight doesn't come from the mind alone. It's deeply felt with a compassionate heart. It enables us to bear witness to the unnecessary suffering that comes from separating ourselves from our own goodness. I gained confidence in this understanding over years of meeting people in my counseling office. It was a shelter where people who were tumbling through their bardos could find emotional support. I couldn't predict the outcome of the challenges they were grappling with, but I could offer love. My training in graduate school emphasized the importance of staying in relationship with my own suffering instead of trying to push it away or pathologize it. As a result, underneath the stories, I wasn't afraid to feel my clients' pain as no different from my own. I became convinced that it's impossible not to love someone when you listen with an open heart to the stories of their lives. It was easy for me to see their inner beauty but painful to witness the core fears that blinded them from it themselves. These fears are hidden or masked but can be recognized with compassionate understanding.

The insight that comes from an open heart is like a loving grandparent who sees the big picture with panoramic awareness. This pillar of protection can guide our decisions about what to cultivate and what to refrain from as we make our way forward in our bardo journey.

GRANDMOTHER WISDOM

Panoramic awareness is like an elder watching grandchildren building castles in the sand, knowing the children don't realize that the waves will wash their creations away. We feel compassion for their loss, but we also understand what they'll learn from their experience. Applying this to our bardo, with the pillar of insight we can listen and learn from our own ups and downs, hold steady and stay in relationship with the goodness that is always present.

Grandmother wisdom responds to suffering with compassion but isn't fooled by stories that mask our fear. This grandmother sees all the way through to our heart, to the story behind the story. She's accommodating and affectionate, hearing our story without criticism or judgment. When we find this loving wisdom within us, we can do two things at once: We follow the emotional plot line of our stories, the real-life dramas unfolding in our life, while appreciating the humanity, the basic goodness, of the actors who are playing their roles. With insight we can begin to recognize the way we freeze other people when we trap them in our personal projections, not allowing them to be simply who they are. As we unmask our core fears, we open the channel of communication with others as well. This is the healing journey that awakening our heart of bodhicitta can illuminate.

When thinking of grandmother wisdom, you don't have to envision your actual grandmother. For instance, my personal image of grandmother wisdom is Virginia Hilliker, my mentor from graduate school. She practiced family therapy until she was well into her nineties, and she had a special interest in child psychology. Virginia showed me how to listen from the heart and restore relationships within family systems to allow intergenerational healing. Her view was that the flow of goodness is never lost; sanity and health is fundamental to who we are. The grandmother figure that inspires you can be anyone who sees your own goodness with wisdom and compassion.

GIVING SPACE TO OUR INNER CHILD

During graduate school I interned as a children's counselor in a shelter for battered women, a neutral zone in a deadly war that's hidden behind closed doors in normal-looking neighborhoods throughout the city. It was hard for me, a student counselor, to find the healthiness in these families disrupted by violence, addiction, and terror. The shelter was like a wartime field hospital. We offered the first level of recovery: personal safety for the victims.

I turned to Virginia for advice because I had no idea how to begin to help the traumatized children in my play-therapy group.

She taught me something that became central to all my family therapy work decades later. "Children are naturally compassionate, willing to exchange their comfort to try to absorb their parents' pain. This is the price they pay to stay in relationship."

Virginia's grandmother eyes saw the innocent origins of our core fears. When we're young children, our hearts are wide open but we lack wisdom. Without the maturity of healthy boundaries, children absorb their parents' pain and weave it into whatever identity will offer relief. For example, if the adult is aggressive, the child may take on the blame and create a false sense of self around the core belief that they're unforgivable. If the child is ignored or neglected, they respond by suppressing their need for attention and buy into the core fear that they don't belong, that they are unwelcome. If the parent needs to win, the child will adapt by seeing themselves as a loser.

This inner lost child is the part of ourselves that comes to these wrong conclusions. We were born with the survival need to stay in a relationship at all costs. Our inner child's heart is open, and as a result we willingly exchange our well-being to take on the suffering of others. This trade-off explains how some of our core fears continue from childhood throughout our life, hidden behind a mistaken idea of who we are. If we want to stay in relationship with someone who believes they're more important than we are, we take on the role of being unworthy. We unconsciously agree to be unworthy to keep that person in our life because the worst thing that could happen to any human being is to be shunned out of existence.

THIS IS NOT WHO YOU ARE

One day I met with Virginia because I was feeling hopeless. I showed up at the shelter that morning and learned that two of the children I'd been working with had disappeared during the night, fleeing with their mother back to the war zone. When I shared this with Virginia, she turned around, opened a drawer in her desk, and brought out a tiny mirror. She held it up and asked if I could see my reflection. Yes, I could. "It doesn't matter how little time you have with a child," she explained. "If you were able to reflect their goodness back, show them that you see who they really are, they will never forget it."

Virginia looked at everyone with grandmother eyes, seeing the story of a tender child behind our frozen heart stories. She could reach through, touching our self-doubt. She conveyed a confident reassurance, "I know that's not who you are." With grandmother eyes we see through the outer plot lines of our stories and attune to the inner tender meaning behind them. If we've discovered this authenticity within ourselves, we can be a guide to others because we recognize frozen fear. We know how it feels, how it tastes, and how it deceives us. Simply recognizing frozen fear brings the warmth of compassion that can melt it back to the original tenderness of our heart. Whatever version of the outer story being told, the wise grandmother is always attuned to the lost child, and their core fear, behind the mask.

When we're lost in our projections, we need someone who can point out what is true and what is not true; someone who reminds us, "You're okay; you're basically good." It's more than hearing it; it's unmasking our fear as an innocent misunderstanding.

PATH OF HEALING

Core fear is a background anxiety. With grandmother eyes we look for the origin of this fear, asking where we got the idea that there's something wrong with who we are. The path of healing is both psychological and spiritual. First, we need to develop healthy boundaries so that we can see clearly. A healthy boundary isn't the armoring of frozen fear; it's the clarity of grandmother eyes, knowing the difference between what nourishes us and what poisons us.

Spiritual healing supports that openness by training with mindfulness, awareness, and compassion. As adults, we can compassionately exchange ourselves for others with the clarity and unconditional love that we lacked as young children. But first we need to heal ourselves.

When emotional storms show up in our bardo, we need to open our heart, listen, and bring ourselves home gently, with reassurance. Grandmother love is the insight that connects with our inner lost child and releases us from the fear that we're fundamentally broken. Seeing through to our basic goodness, we make the wish that all beings would never be separated from this great happiness, the true nature of our heart, free from confusion.

Contemplation
NAMING YOUR CORE FEAR

- What do you think of as your core fear? Here are five examples: *I'm afraid I'm unlovable. I'm afraid I'm unforgivable. I'm afraid I'm unwelcome. I'm afraid I'm powerless. I'm afraid I'm unworthy.*
- How might these core fears be an intelligent but innocent misunderstanding in response to the kinds of early relationships you were in?
- Do you remember a time in your early childhood when you tried to comfort an adult's distress? If so, can you witness this with your own "grandmother eyes"?

Meditation

BEING A LOVING GRANDMOTHER

10 MINUTES

Here is a personal practice of exchange that we can do to heal our version of a core fear.

Begin by setting the intention of the third limitless one: *May I and all beings not be separated from the great happiness, discovering our basic goodness, free of suffering.*

If you like, you can place a photo of your younger self on a chair in front of you. Or you can use your imagination.

Feel your adult self as like a loving grandmother, with dignity, clarity, and love. Imagine a beautiful moon in your heart radiating outward.

In front, you see your suffering in the image of a lost child—whatever that means for you at this moment.

This child might represent vulnerable feelings of shame or embarrassment. The child might say, "I'm not good enough; I'm not worthy; I'll never be forgivable." Hear your own words for your hidden fears.

This is an embodied practice, so the visualization and the words are invitations to feel a connection in your body.

As the loving grandmother with a sense of this lost child in front of you, go back to feeling the moon in your heart radiating. Just feel that.

Now as you breathe out, extend your arms and connect with that lost child.

(continued)

Then on the in-breath, embrace that lost child; fold your arms to bring that child into your heart.

Repeat this again. Extending and radiating with the out-breath. Once again you are listening to that lost child, and maybe there's a different message this time. Maybe the child is saying, "I've never been welcome, I've never belonged."

Again, you touch that vulnerable feeling and breathe it into your heart, into the moon in your heart.

Repeat this one more time, extending out, connecting, and then bringing that child home. Feel this reunion of your adult self, like a loving grandmother, as it melts the fear of your inner lost child.

Do this practice of extending and embracing three times and then simply rest. Don't judge or criticize how you do this practice. It doesn't have to be perfect. Just holding up a little mirror is enough. Trust that there's something restorative that is occurring in this embodied practice. This lost child is who we've been turning away from our whole life. We've been lost, and now there's a pathway home.

The wisdom of all these teachings is realizing that the space for healing is always occurring in the present moment. It doesn't require a long history. It can be a 100 percent in this moment. The fact that you lose it again a moment later doesn't matter because it's always returning. That's one of the beautiful things about this path—it's a restorative journey.

17

Patience

When we're putting up the barriers and the sense of "me" as separate from "you" gets stronger, right there in the midst of difficulty and pain, the whole thing could turn around simply by *not erecting barriers*; simply by staying open to the difficulty, to the feelings that you're going through; simply by not talking to ourselves about what's happening.

—Pema Chödrön, *Practicing Peace in Times of War*

The first three pillars of protection—kindness circle, self-compassion, and insight—are foundational and increase our sensitivity to the impact that our communication has on other people. The fourth pillar, patience, requires looking beyond ourselves with grandmother eyes to protect the core fears we might be triggering in others. To do this, we need to hold steady at the tipping point when our heart is about to freeze. This is supported by the aspiration to keep our heart open so that we and others may "dwell in the great equanimity, free from passion, aggression, and prejudice."

This teaching on the "great equanimity" reminds us that everyone we meet has the same tender heart, the same basic goodness, as we do. Before our walls go up, this goodness is the unspoken energy that flows between us. It is love. We protect this flow of connection with patience.

When I officiate weddings, I always remind the couple that the vows they're taking aren't for the times when they feel in love. Rather, they're reminders to be patient in the storms that will inevitably come. (As a couples counselor, I've seen what those emotional storms look like.) But we don't need to be in an intimate relationship to keep our heart open. Practicing bodhicitta, we can learn to meet opportunities in every encounter we have.

Patience is essential in a bardo because we never know who we will be relying on for help. Our friends or family might not be available, and a stranger might be the person who steps forward to hold our hand. This is why it's important to keep the channel of communication open during difficult times. Of all the ways that we transform fear into love, patience is one of the most immediate and powerful tools we have.

We all know how it feels when an emotional reaction suddenly flares up. This is the time when we need to pause and notice that we're at a tipping point. We can ask ourselves, "Do I want to cut off the flow of communication or stay with it? Am I about to inflict pain to make my point?" This tipping point is a moment of clarity that can make or break a relationship.

HOPE AND FEAR

When you're in a bardo, it can feel like you're walking around with no skin. Everything touches you deeply. Most of the time you feel the goodness of strangers, but sometimes you're hurt by other people's fear. I remember a client in grief after the death of her son saying that a friend approaching on the sidewalk crossed the street to avoid meeting her. When your heart is broken, you feel a heightened contrast between open and closed communication.

One afternoon around the midpoint of my chemotherapy treatment, I had a chance to watch my reactions at this tipping point.

It was hard to go out in public when I was bald. I wore a cap, but it couldn't hide my feeling of nakedness. I was looking out at the world with painfully dry eyes and no eyebrows or eyelashes. I felt as though the words *cancer patient* were written on my forehead. But in the pandemic bardo, we mostly glided past one another without making an impression. That sterile environment intensified a childlike need in me to belong, to be greeted by someone who would recognize my situation with kindness, like a stray animal needing to be welcomed into a pack. At the same time, I feared being shunned. Both happened on the same day during my first visit back to the grocery store.

The welcoming connection was only momentary and wordless, but it was a message sent and received with love. I couldn't see her face behind the mask, but a woman paused and looked at me in a way that broadcasted that she understood what I was going through. She said nothing, but I instantaneously felt held by her compassionate presence. It meant the world to me at that moment.

Later, in the slow, socially distanced checkout line, my phone rang. It was a friend returning a call. After a short exchange to catch up on the year or so since we'd talked, I mentioned that I had called her to ask for some help at home because I had breast cancer. There was a short silence and then she abruptly hung up. I had forgotten how afraid she was of sickness and death.

Later, reflecting on these exchanges, I realized that the vulnerability that I felt upon entering the grocery store, the feeling of nakedness before my self-consciousness arose, is the texture of "great equanimity." It was briefly there, pausing at the threshold before I projected the drama that cast some people as potential allies, others as enemies, and the rest as unimportant. At that moment I felt openhearted and curious, with no sense of barriers between us. The grocery store was a pool of tender human beings sending and receiving in an unspoken flow of communication. I had been contemplating this bodhicitta practice for years, but now those words came to life. *May we dwell in the great equanimity, free from trying to pull others in with passion, or aggressively rejecting them.* This is the truth that is there before the prejudice of a frozen fear barrier goes up. It is this vulnerability, this boundless heart-space we all share, that makes it possible for us to be patient with one another. Without tenderness, trying to be patient is an uphill grind. But when we feel the space between us as goodness, we have a chance to pause, tune in to that vulnerability, and open right at the moment when we are about to freeze. The pillar of patience, supporting the tender heart of limitless love, makes our relationships resilient.

TIPPING POINTS

Patience is meeting our edge when stress triggers us to react to the people around us. We might lash out angrily or put up a wall of silent resentment. When we feel emotionally hungry, we might ask someone to do more for us than they can. My teacher's words ring true: without the ups and downs of our relationships with other people, we could never learn to be patient.

Patience protects our emotional intelligence. If we know to listen, our emotions tell us what we need. When we're lonely, we need company. When we're sad, we need comfort. When we're afraid, we need reassurance. If we can communicate these emotional needs to the people around us, they can help us through our dark times. The problem is that we lose touch with this emotional intelligence when we shut down.

Without patience, reactive emotions flare up like a fever. Aggression, paranoia, or depression can take over. This is dangerous in a bardo because we're at risk of cutting ourselves off from the people we depend on. So, the first tool we need to strengthen patience is to recognize tipping points that remind us that we're in danger. The teachings direct us to three main tipping points: craving, aggression, and prejudice.

Beyond Craving

The first tipping point, when the barrier of frozen fear rises, is emotional hunger—wanting to pull people into our territory. What we don't see is that the cause of this suffering is the illusion that we're cut off from the nourishment we need. Emotional hunger is passion, or craving, rather than true friendship. It's self-centered, wanting others to make us happy or relieve us of our discomfort. This tipping point happened to me at the grocery store when I started to feel self-conscious about looking odd, like a cancer patient. This triggered a need to belong. In other circumstances, this need might have become more demanding, craving attention or love with unrealistic expectations.

Beyond Aggression

The second tipping point is aggression, pushing people away when they seem to threaten us. When my friend hung up the phone on me, I flipped into thinking of her as an enemy because I felt hurt. I could have retaliated by trying to ruin her reputation with our mutual friends, telling them how cruel she was. For an instant, my reactions were all about me: "How dare she not want to help me."

Beyond Prejudice

The third tipping point is prejudice—that is, "pre-judging," the habit of dehumanizing and not caring about others one way or another. The frozen-fear barrier is kept in place by a closed mind. I've seen myself do this countless times, but in my example story, it was my friend who shut down when she heard the word *cancer*. Fear seized control over her mind, and she hung up the phone. When we're in a bardo, frozen fear often controls our decision-making, silencing input from friends or family—even medical experts—who see our situation more clearly. We might do the opposite, sinking into a helpless bewilderment and letting others make decisions for us. I've seen friends go for second, third, fourth opinions from doctors without being able to make up their mind about how to proceed with their cancer treatment.

I suggest imagining a red light to remind us to hit the brakes when we feel these tipping points triggering us to shut down. We can train in advance by becoming familiar with these red-light signals and the scripts in our mind that justify freezing the space between us.

LEARNING TO STOP, LOOK, LISTEN!

In my work with couples, we used the green-light and red-light symbols as an aid to recognize the difference in how it feels when we're open to communication in contrast to when we're closed.

When we're open, our basic sanity is like a green light, indicating that we can trust our curiosity and vulnerability. When we're frozen, we think of a red light, a warning signal that we're at risk because we're not able to listen.

There are three steps in practicing patience using these traffic-light symbols: stop, look, and listen.

Stop: A Warning Signal

Stop is learning to notice the tipping points when we freeze the openhearted space between us. The best protection from damaging our relationships is creating space to listen to our words before we say them out loud.

The stop signal reminds us to refrain from causing harm. It signals for us to stop: Delete that text we're about to send. Turn off the phone. Now it's time to try something new. Take a shower. Interrupt the momentum. Stop.

When I'm in that state of mind, I truly believe that I need to win, to get that last word in; or I blame Jerry for something I later discover wasn't his fault. In the grip of frozen fear, I'm always right, he's always wrong.

Look: With Grandmother Eyes

Look is remembering to see with grandmother eyes, noticing the core fear we're triggering in the other person. Are we keeping the bridge of connection open or are we putting up a wall? We're waking up to the big picture, seeing that we can either interrupt a chain reaction of suffering or keep it going.

This second step is the most important. It's time to look through to the other side of that barrier and see the expression on the other person's face. Consider the impact your words would have on the other person. What's the price we're paying to inflate ourselves at this person's expense? What's the story behind the story? What is it that I really want? What's the pain underneath this other person's mask?

Listen: With Love

Listen means that instead of defending our territory, we can listen to our heart and trade *me* for *we*, melting the barrier and joining with the other person. It's possible to melt blame into mercy or jealousy into admiration on the spot.

When we bring compassion to the core fears that we're triggering in another person, we're simultaneously feeling the pain of our own core fear, self-doubt in our own basic goodness. Remember, another person's core fears fit hand in glove with the negative messages we deliver. When we act out our projections, we're replaying our own origin story. But if we listen to ourselves and look at the expression of who we're talking to, we can awaken empathy and return to the wide-open, tender space of equanimity. We think, "Where did I get the idea that the way to protect myself is to hurt this person?" Feel that tender vulnerability.

The teachings on bodhicitta say that we can dwell in a *great equanimity beyond passion, aggression, and ignorance.* This is the view from our basic sanity, our authentic self, which is there before we freeze people into objects to meet our own needs. Few of us remember these teachings all day long, but we can learn to trust the feeling of being vulnerable. When I entered the grocery store, this tenderness was like ground zero. If I were to pause and simply remember the feeling of that space, it had a quality of loneliness but at the same time a sense of being open to whatever interactions were about to occur.

Contemplation

DWELLING IN EQUANIMITY

- Recall your own red-light signals when frozen fear arises and you're afraid to expose your vulnerable feelings—the pain of needing to belong, the hope for approval, the pain of being rejected. What does it feel like in your body when you shut down this pain? What does it feel like in your heart when its unsafe to be vulnerable? What happens to your mind when you are silenced?

- Now, take a moment to feel and consider your experiences with love. Have you experienced feeling accepted for being exactly who you are? What does it feel like to be loved? Expand on this inquiry by also answering in the following ways: What does it feel like in your body to be loved? What does it feel like to open your heart to being loved? What happens to your mind when you feel loved?

Meditation
TIPPING POINTS
10 MINUTES

This practice is another version of exchanging self for other. It's raising our compassionate awareness to notice the way our frozen-fear patterns trigger our listener's core fear. When we do this, we're freezing the space between us, turning the other person into an object. The practice is to hold steady right at that tipping point, relax, and open to the space of equanimity.

Sit for five minutes. Next, reflect on the fourth limitless one: *May I and all beings dwell in the great equanimity free from passion, aggression, and ignorance.*

Passion: Ask yourself, "When I disrespect someone's boundaries out of my own emotional hunger, am I triggering their core fear of feeling devoured instead of loved?"

(continued)

Now, melt the barrier; flip the script of craving someone's attention, melt the core fear by giving space to the relationship.

Holding your hands to your heart, imagine saying these words: "I love and appreciate who you are, as you are."

Extending your hands with the out-breath, touch the pain of addictive craving.

Bringing your hands back to your heart with the in-breath, feel the space of unconditional acceptance. *May I and all beings dwell in the great equanimity free from addictive craving.*

Aggression: Ask yourself, "When I'm aggressive with someone, am I triggering them to feel at fault or unforgivable?"

Now, melt the barrier; flip the script of blame, restore mercy and forgiveness to this core wound.

Holding your hands to your heart; on the in-breath, imagine saying these words: "My criticism or blame has nothing do with you. I'm sorry."

Extending your hands with the out-breath, touch the pain of a blaming mind.

Bringing your hands back to your heart, feel the limitless space of love. *May I and all beings dwell in the great equanimity free from aggression.*

Ignorance: Ask yourself, "When I'm shunning, ignoring, or giving a cold shoulder, am I triggering someone to feel unwelcome or invisible?"

Now, melt the barrier; flip the script of ignoring, restore loving attention to this core fear.

Holding your hands to your heart, imagine saying these words: "You are always welcome."

Extending your hands with the out-breath, touch the pain of ignorance in all its forms.

Bringing your hands back to your heart, rest in the limitless space that cherishes all beings with equal value. *May I and all beings dwell in the great equanimity free from prejudice.*

Create your own version of these or other negative scripts associated with painful reactions so they're easy to catch. When they show up in your communication, even in your mind, imagine flagging them with a warning signal, such as a mental image of a flashing red light. Pause, flip the script, and embrace the goodness of great equanimity.

18

Rainbow after the Storm

Like light passing through a crystal, bodhicitta radiates in many hues and directions.

—Khenpo Palden Sherab, *Door to Inconceivable Wisdom and Compassion*

This chapter will conclude the middle phase of our bardo. Like storm chasers, we've been in the eye of the hurricane, looking directly into our personal experience of painful emotions. If we don't suppress them or act them out, there's wisdom in these energies that can illuminate a moment of choice, the tipping point where frozen fear can melt into fearlessness. This is how we finally see through the patterns that make our painful emotions seem real. Healing our emotional suffering is a process of softening and opening to groundlessness rather than holding on to familiar territory. A bardo is the perfect time to learn this.

The COVID-19 lockdown and the cancer diagnosis ended ten years of nonstop teaching and traveling. I wasn't used to time off. I felt like that cartoon of the coyote who keeps running in the air just before falling off a cliff. Suddenly everything stopped. I had permission to feel my exhaustion and finally rest.

I started to take afternoon naps in our sunny bedroom, where crystals dangled in the window, creating rainbows that danced along the walls. Jerry and I laughed at our cat when he tried to catch these plays of light. As I lay there, drifting in and out of sleep, with music softly playing in the background, the dreamlike quality of my life felt like those rainbows. Sometimes I was the cat, believing they were real, coming up with strategies to attack or hold them. At other times I was able to see their transparency and enjoy the play of light.

I imagine that dying will be like waking up from a dream. Everything that seemed so real, so vivid and compelling, will dissolve. What remains, it seems, would be the play of light. At least this is what the bardo teachings tell us. Along with that, there will be awareness and love, because bodhicitta doesn't die; it isn't centralized in our body or brain.

MELTING FEAR INTO LOVE

A rainbow is sometimes used to describe the two qualities of awakened heart: wisdom and love. The space of wisdom is the clear light of clarity, the *great equanimity*. We experience that space by opening to our vulnerability, the tenderness of our heart. The true nature of our emotions is like a play of colors that we feel and perceive but cannot grasp. This sensitivity is always present in the background of our experience, even though we often overlook it. As we've seen, frozen fear is the habit of turning away from vulnerability, triggered by the fear that it's a weakness rather than a strength.

With the support of the four pillars and the bodhicitta practice of the four limitless wishes, it's possible to turn toward this tender heart, meet our fears, unmask the painful emotions that cover it up, and finally melt that fear back into love. The groundlessness of a bardo gives us an opportunity to discover this warrior path for ourselves.

We began our journey in part one with the shocking news that we're all going to die, and it can happen at any moment without warning. My cancer diagnosis was a wake-up call for me at first, but then it lulled me back to sleep again. Imagining that I would die of cancer at some future time closed my eyes to the possibility that I might die in a car accident today. So, throughout my journey I needed to keep reminding myself that death comes without warning, that everything we cherish can disappear in a heartbeat. Waking up again and again to this realization isn't cause for depression. It is the crack in our armor that can bring us home to the great equanimity, the tender space of our natural heart.

Accepting the truth of impermanence gives our life a dreamlike quality. Like a rainbow, sooner or later the people, homes, and things we cherish will disappear from our life. At the same time, something new is arising every moment. This truth is both terrifying and liberating. It's terrifying when we're like the little child at the party who panics because they've forgotten that they're sitting in her mother's lap. It's liberating when we can let go, turn around, and come home to the truth that love without grasping is limitless.

TOUCH AND GO

Cancer has made life worth living. Keeping death in mind has had a healing effect on my relationships, especially with my partner, Jerry. We've weathered many emotional storms, but I didn't anticipate that our relationship would blossom over the year of my cancer treatment. Thanks to his sense of humor and patience, I've been able to see for myself that love is more fundamental to our nature than fear. When I'm about to fall into one of my reactive patterns, like the cat trying to grab hold of a rainbow, Jerry is a compassionate mirror. He reflects but doesn't play into my game. Without a reaction on his part, I see the truth: "That's frozen fear, the cause of suffering."

Like a rainbow, our experience is both real and unreal at the same time. The way to relate to this is by touching with affection but being willing to let go. Normally when we use the phrase "touch and go," it is a cause for concern. When we ask how a friend in the ICU is doing and we hear "touch and go," it's not reassuring. But in the paradoxical wisdom of the Buddhist teachings, this is the best way to understand the nature of love.

The world is floating; everything we experience is in flux. Scientists can witness this dynamic space through microscopes and telescopes. They can prove to us that everything is impermanent—touch and go. What the Buddha contributes is the good news, that this touch and go is the energy of our heart, the play of love and wisdom.

Love is touching, fully appreciating the beauty of the present moment, and feeling grateful to the people in our lives. Wisdom is letting go into space, the bigger mind that knows when we're dreaming.

Contemplation
A PATH OF TENDERNESS

- Looking back on part two, reflect on your experience of applying the teachings on bodhicitta as a support for working with your emotions.
- What is your personal experience of turning toward vulnerability?
- What do you understand to be the relationship between letting go of grasping and finding a greater appreciation of people as they are?
- Thinking of your bardo experiences, how do these times in your life show you the truth of impermanence?

Meditation

WAKING FROM A DREAM

UP TO 10 MINUTES

Like a crystal, the white light of wisdom refracts into rainbows as a display of compassion. The bardo teachings tell us that this is a display of the true nature of our emotions when we're liberated into love. To bring this teaching into daily life, here is a meditation for waking up from a dream.

Whenever possible, practice this meditation during the transition between sleeping and waking up, upon awakening in the morning or from a nap. If you can do this with your eyes still closed, that would be best. Remain lying in bed and take a few minutes to pause before getting up.

Minutes ago, you were asleep, possibly dreaming. Allow some time to feel this little bardo dissolving, touching the dream, remembering what remains of the colors and activities and the dream body that was real for you.

Put your hand on your heart and feel the emotions that were stirred up in your dream stories. Touch them gently and then watch them go.

Gradually, as you wake up further, allow your dream self to dissolve like a rainbow into a spacious state of mind. Your waking thoughts and emotions aren't organized yet. Just rest in that in-between space for a moment.

Put your other hand on your belly and feel the rise and fall of your breath. Feel a sense of being embodied, as if for the first time.

As you awake further, set your intention to be present, kind, and willing to face whatever situations you will be in today with an open mind and heart.

Move from Core Fear to Compassionate Rebirth

Any positive energy we put toward ourselves or others creates an atmosphere of love and compassion that ripples out and out—who knows how far? With this in mind, we could come to this exploration of death with our best self, the self that is sensitive to the fears and pains of our fellow beings and wants to help.

—Pema Chödrön, *How We Live Is How We Die*

T he lesson reinforced by my cancer bardo is that we human beings are incredibly resilient when our suffering is embraced by
love. This doesn't mean that it magically goes away but that we can
learn to stay awake, listen, and pay attention rather than shutting
down. Our hearts know how to spontaneously open when a community gathers after a disaster or we meet in grief support groups
after a loss. Listening openly, letting go of judgment and preconceived ideas, we discover the healing power of seeing one another
for who we are.

We began our bardo journey in part one with the shock of
awake fear, a rude awakening to the truth of impermanence.
To stay awake, we learn to listen to our body with the practice
of mindfulness. Our body is always grounded in the present moment, like a nurturing mother's presence, holding us steady with
loving-kindness: "I see you, I feel you, I'm here with you." The
truth that our body will die at some future time can wake us up to
the joy of being alive today. We can hear this joy in people, like my
friend Kim, who know how to nourish themselves by drinking in
moments of beauty and gratefully receiving love from friends and
strangers alike.

In part two we entered the emotional storms triggered by frozen fear, the defensive habit of avoiding real or imaginary threats
by walling ourselves off from others. We explored the causes of
emotional suffering as the habit of turning away from our vulnerability, cutting ourselves off from the roots of happiness and our
interdependence with one another. As a result, we're confused
about who we are. We identify with stories and opinions that trigger reactive emotions rather than with our sensitive feelings. As
our bardo guide, we envisioned a wise grandmother with the compassionate wisdom to see through our mask to our worthiness. We
protected the bridge of bodhicitta with four pillars to support us in
crossing over the treacherous patterns of frozen fear.

In part three, we turn toward the background anxiety of our core fear, which, like a neglected wound, only harms us because we don't examine it. The core fear is doubt in our intrinsic goodness. We're not sure who we are, so we fill in the gap with a false self, a feeling of being unworthy or undeserving of love. The practice of meditation and self-reflection gives us a chance to discover that we are born from love and return to love. This is how we're reborn into a new normal that's liberated from fear. We might imagine our guide through this final stage of our bardo as being like a midwife. Loving eyes see our original innocence: "I know who you are."

COMPASSIONATE ACTION

When we awaken to the truth, we see our human nature as the great equanimity of basic goodness. This tender reality can leave us feeling heartbroken. Opening our eyes to the suffering of the world, we can feel overwhelmed. We wish we had the power to cure cancer, reverse climate change, protect the vulnerable, or end all wars. There's so much pain out there. But the bardo teachings have shown us that we have power: it's possible to melt fear and open our heart with love. As a childhood friend once said, "The big things weigh me down, but the little things lift me up."

The Buddhist practice of the four limitless ones has been our guide, protected by the pillars of friendship, self-compassion, insight, and patience. Step by step, opening our heart to our fear and suffering, we recognize how frozen barriers dissolve when we come home to our true nature—basic goodness. Now, in the final stage of our healing journey we will explore four qualities of an awakened heart: tenderness, sadness, mercy, and fearlessness. Motivated by love, we can be reborn with these powers of compassion that enable us to interrupt the escalation of confusion and aggression in our relationships.

REBIRTH: A NEW IDENTITY

The bardo teachings tell us that there are two motivating forces that determine our rebirth after death. We're either driven by mindlessness—clinging to our defensive reactions—or by the compassionate wish to help others. This compassionate wish is like a loving mother who can't be free until she's rescued her child. With an awakened heart, in the space of great equanimity, we see that child in everyone. This is the traditional interpretation of this last phase of the bardo. How do we apply these teachings to our bardos in everyday life? Rather than thinking of rebirth as a one-time occurrence and a literal event, we can practice with our turning points, noticing how metaphorical rebirths happen throughout our life. Looking back, we can learn from those difficult periods that intensified our fear but also opened us to love. And our present and future bardos can be opportunities to use these lessons to help others.

MINDLESS REBIRTH

Mindless rebirth happens all the time when we carry forward our past opinions, mental stories, and emotions as a defensive suit of armor. These repeated patterns determine the environment of the next situation we find ourselves in. For example, an angry person creates an angry world. Inside our suit of armor, our nakedness feels uncomfortable. We might feel the inauthenticity of this false self as a haunting sense that we're an impostor. We're afraid to look inside, take off our armor, and investigate.

Frozen fear blocks us from taking a closer look. What is it that we're so afraid to see? Or feel? We can observe this habit in our mind whenever we choose to look. With self-compassion and insight, we can see this habit of denial as the cause of suffering. Denial neglects the wound of our core fears. With each spin of our defensive patterns, we bypass the opportunity to heal.

Compassionate Rebirth

Earlier in the book, we learned that with self-compassion we can compost our own suffering rather than throwing it away. This is the essential instruction for a compassionate rebirth. Like composting our leftovers, meeting our suffering with love is an ongoing process. But there is a point when we realize that our bardo is coming to an end and we're ready to walk out the door. It's like stepping into the first sunny day after a long rainy spell. It's so bright that we might want to close our eyes, but the sun feels so warm and welcoming that we have no choice but to go forward.

The bardo teachings urge us not to be afraid of our own brilliance, the affectionate relationship we can have with our body, heart, world—every moment of our human life. When we experience the shock of loss in the warmth of loving-kindness and self-compassion, we don't have to freeze. This is how our rebirth can be transformative rather than traumatic. Each time we turned toward our neglected wounds with love, we uncovered the power of our vulnerability. When we emerge from our dark night of the soul, we're reborn into a new normal with the wish to shine a light into that tunnel to help others.

Compassionate actions arise spontaneously, without a plan or strategy. They are a flowering of the seeds we nourished with our bodhicitta aspirations. In our rebirth, our sense of identity has shifted from the lost child to the loving mother. Because we've turned toward our fear and suffering, compassion arises naturally when we encounter the suffering of others. This is the final truth of our journey, the paradoxical wisdom that we're both alone and yet indelibly connected to one another at the heart level. This is why composting our suffering can transform it into the power to be there for others.

19

Quiet Time for Healing

The Buddhists talk about samsara, the world of illusion. It is the place that most of us live. Mistaking illusion for reality is said to be the root cause of our suffering. Yet in some immensely elegant way, suffering itself can release us from illusion.

—Rachel Naomi Remen, *Kitchen Table Wisdom*

In mid-December 2020, I had my last infusion of chemo followed by the final week of daily self-injections to coax my white blood cells back to life. I'd crawled to the finish line of this second phase of treatment and had a month to rebuild my immune system before starting radiation. I had no idea who this woman in the mirror was, bloated and ruddy-cheeked, with no hair, eyelashes, or toenails.

I followed the news that a vaccine for the COVID-19 pandemic was on the horizon, but people were dying by the thousands every day. Unimaginable waves of grief were flooding families and communities. And we were still so isolated. How can we hold each other when we're out of reach?

The weight of the pandemic was straining our social infrastructures too. Hospitals and supply chains were near a breaking point. Ominously, in the background, another kind of virus was spreading. The culture of fear was on the rise, and toxic propaganda streaming through the internet was feeding lonely, isolated people with hateful conspiracies.

THE POWER OF LOVING PRESENCE

Conversation is essential because human beings are interdependent, nourished by relationship. Even a short chat with a stranger in the elevator can replenish our supply of love. Love circulates through our day with small acts of generosity, like the driver who waves our car into a space in traffic. Receiving kindness inspires us to pay it forward; we look for opportunities to help someone else out. Every time we open our heart—listening, paying attention to someone else—we're contributing to the flow of goodness that keeps our relationships and communities resilient.

Dr. Martin Luther King Jr. famously proclaimed the power of love to interrupt hate: "I have decided to stick with love. Hate is too great a burden to bear."[4] His intention was the anchor for a culture of nonviolence, a callout to the goodness of our nature. A few years ago, I came across another example of that kind of heroism. I've shared this story in my classes, including in a lecture at a peace conference in Vienna. It's a true-life parable about the power of loving presence to interrupt someone else's aggressive escalation.

It began one August morning in 2013, when Michael Hill, in a deranged fit of despair, decided that today would be the day he would die. His plan included taking as many others as he could with him, a violent outburst that would end with suicide by police. He loaded his assault rifle and headed for an elementary school. The last thing he expected was that he'd be rescued by love.

Michael Hill took Antoinette Tuff, the school bookkeeper, as his hostage. As Gary Younge wrote in the *Guardian*, Antoinette was able to successfully negotiate between Michael and the police:

"We're not going to hate you," she said, referring to him first as "sir" and later as "sweetie" and "baby." "My pastor, he just started this teaching on resting, and how you anchor yourself in the Lord," recalled Tuff, who said she was terrified. "I just sat there and started praying."

And so in between updates with the 911 dispatcher she shared her own travails with Hill, telling him about her divorce and disabled son, all the while reassuring him. "I love you. I'm proud of you. We all go through something in life. You're gonna be OK. Sweetheart. I tried to commit suicide last year after my husband left me." Eventually, while keeping police at a distance, she persuaded him to give up his weapons, lie on the floor and give himself up.[5]

To try to understand Antoinette's compassion, I wanted to learn more about her suicidal crisis, her personal bardo journey. How had she worked with her pain after her husband left her the year before her story exploded into the news? In my counseling office, I've witnessed a lot of suffering, but the pain of betrayal is one of the hardest. As one of my clients in a similar situation once said, "I feel like I'm boiling in hot oil. I would kill myself, but I don't want to give him the satisfaction."

Betrayal is a painful and dangerous bardo. To protect our heart, we need to be careful about what voices we listen to. If we're left listening solely to our core fear—that we're unlovable or unworthy, for instance—then we are on our own, lost, clinging to the past, hungry for love, falling into despair, and unable to see a future. Our emotional immune system is out of whack, and we can be infected by resentments and blame. Misguided emotions tied to our core fear might drive us to harm ourselves, to destroy the reputation of the person we once loved, anything to escape the pain. It feels like we're out of control, bumping around on a plane that's crashing into a dark sea below. I learned that Antoinette chose a different route. She met her despair by anchoring in her heart, transforming her personal suffering into the power of compassion.

QUIET TIME AS A FORMULA FOR HEALING

Antoinette was able to talk through the gunman's rage because she understood the frozen fear that was driving it. Antoinette had turned her suicidal crisis around by creating time to listen to her heart. The morning of the shooting, and every morning for the past year, she had begun her day reading her Bible, pouring her heart out in words to God, and listening silently. Her pastor called this "quiet time." I recognized her contemplative dialogue as similar to the tonglen of self-compassion, touching our pain and then opening space to listen.

Antoinette anchored her heart with compassion in three steps. First, she turned to her Bible for guidance. Then she prayed out loud, finding words to express her pain. Finally, for an equal amount of time, she was quiet, creating a listening space that held her pain rather than acting it out. With these three practices she was able to not only embrace her trauma with love but also extend her loving presence to someone else amid their crisis.

This daily practice created an inner calm that kept Antoinette awake despite her fear and gave her the only two weapons she would need: her words and her compassion. She stayed in relationship with Michael as a person, not as an enemy. This is the freedom that comes from listening to our suffering with love. Later Antoinette said, "I may not have known his name, but I sure knew his pain. In fact, I understand his pain—his fear and his anger and his hopelessness and his sad, pleading wish to just cease to be—better than he could have ever known."[6]

Throughout the crisis, Antoinette's unspoken message to Michael was loving presence: "I see you; I feel you, I'm here with you."

She recognized cracks in his psychological armor, those short interruptions when his humanity was unmasked. When someone is in a deranged state of mind, they're operating from the most primitive part of the brain. With little interruptions, it's possible to snap them out of it. It was as though Antoinette reached through those gaps and spoke directly to his vulnerability, as a mother would to a son trapped in prison. She saw through the outer image of a violent gunman and allowed a tender, frightened young man to emerge. She was like a martial artist who could lean into the energy of aggression and flip it around.

In the final moments of the crisis, Antoinette abruptly cut through Michael's aggression in a stroke of spontaneous fearlessness. She had tried to persuade him that he could surrender, but he replied that it was too late, his plan had gone too far. It was as if she was a wise grandmother waking a child up from a nightmare.

During those last few days of 2020, I thought about Antoinette and her unintentional heroism. The new year was approaching, my chemotherapy was finally over, but the COVID-19 pandemic was still raging. I saw how isolation was freezing the narratives of suffering from despair into hatred. I said to myself, "No, this isn't how the story has to end." I wanted to turn my isolation into quiet time, to incubate the seeds of compassion with the wish to be of benefit to others in any way possible.

FOUR COMPASSIONATE POWERS

Spontaneous compassion is the flowering of the seeds nourished by the practice of the four bodhicitta aspirations that we worked with in part two. Step by step, in our own version of Antoinette's quiet time, we've been deepening our intention to meet unexpected situations with an open heart. The groundlessness of my cancer bardo was an opportunity to relate with fear directly. But how does the energy of fear melt into confidence, and where does the power of compassion come from? To understand this, let's turn to four qualities of bodhicitta: tenderness, sadness, mercy, and fearlessness. I envisioned these as the four compassionate powers.

Tenderness: Touching the Wound

We can see the first compassionate power as Antoinette's ability to be present, drawing strength from tenderness. With the eyes of unconditional loving-kindness, we can see who people really are. If we're able to stay awake with our own fear, we can attune to the basic goodness of others as a shared, felt presence. This tenderness is the touchstone for all our relationships. It's a yearning to communicate, to understand, to give and receive love.

Sadness: A Heart-to-Heart Bridge

The second compassionate power is bearing witness to the suffering of frozen fear, holding steady with sadness instead of reacting one way or another. Antoinette understood Michael's despair better than he did. She was like a wounded healer, someone who had met her own pain with compassion and as a result was unafraid to meet that pain in others. When we make the wish that all beings be free from suffering and the causes of suffering, we always begin with ourselves. Self-compassion gives us the clarity to see the unnecessary pain caused by the barriers that divide us. We bear witness by making room for both fear and courage to be present at the same time. This quality of sadness, builds a heart-to-heart bridge to connect with others, seeing them as no different from ourselves.

Mercy: No Blame

The third compassionate power is mercy, the quality of the heart that enables us to absorb blame and aggression to keep the channel of communication open. All of Antoinette's messages to Michael had a quality of tonglen—absorbing his pain and extending the message of hope. With mercy, we let go of the logic of retaliation and follow our heart's yearning for reconciliation. We understand that a person's aggression comes from their neglected wounds. There's no need to take it personally. With confidence in our shared basic goodness, we see this fundamental innocence and vulnerability in everything and everyone we meet, from our most intimate friends and partners to strangers.

Fearlessness: Confidence in Goodness

The fourth power of compassion is fearlessness—renouncing the narratives of aggression and trusting in the goodness that is always there, like the sun behind the clouds. When Antoinette abruptly cut through Michael's story, showing him that his version of the last chapter wasn't inevitable, she disarmed him with fearless confidence. Because our bardo journey has brought us face to face with fear, we discover what fearlessness really means. We're free to be there for others. This is the best of our human capacity to make the world a better place. It comes from bringing strength and compassion to our most vulnerable moments so that we can offer the same to others.

Contemplation

MEETING PAIN WITH COMPASSION

- Write about an example from your life when someone was able to free your aggression with compassion in one of these four ways:
  - Tender presence: "I see you, I'm here"; validating your original pain.

(continued)

- Sadness: "I feel your pain"; encouraging, staying connected with empathy.
- Being merciful: absorbing aggression to keep the channel of communication open.
- Interrupting: fearlessly intervening to change the trajectory of your actions.

Meditation

INTERRUPTING YOUR PATTERNS

20 MINUTES

If we can resolve even one crisis of hatred with compassion, this is a huge step. When our barrier comes down, it turns into a bridge, reconnecting us to others and delivering the nourishment we need. The flow of compassion brings the freedom to be tender, merciful, and forgiving. It soothes our wounds and helps us learn from our mishaps.

Set your intention to apply tonglen meditation to interrupt the patterns that escalate anger into hatred. Sit quietly in peaceful meditation for five minutes. Then do the following practice for no more than ten minutes, at your own pace.

Bring a memory to mind that triggers an angry reaction. See the image in your mind, hear the words and feel the tension rising in your body. Let go of focusing on that person and that story and turn your attention inward, to the feeling in your body right now.

Be curious about this emotional energy you are feeling, as if you are reaching into your rib cage, looking for your heart.

Think, "Under my resentment is a tender sadness about having been hurt or threatened by this person. This is the wound that I've been neglecting. If I can stay a bit longer, bringing compassionate curiosity to this wound, I might find that it is not solid. It is made of space, a tender space that is exquisitely sensitive to everything in my environment."

Use this inspiration as your starting point. This is your original heart of bodhicitta—limitless love and power.

Extending your arms with the out-breath, imagine that you are touching the frozen pain of your anger— the tender feelings of hurt, sadness, or grief—that were bypassed when your heart shut down.

On the in-breath, bring your hands to your heart, embracing that pain into the tender, sad, merciful, and fearless space of your basic goodness.

Repeat this three times, then rest.

Whenever the angry story comes back, let go of that thought and gently return to your breath and then return to the practice of extending and embracing again.

Close by sitting again in peaceful meditation for five minutes.

20

Grace

Yes, Mother. . . . I can see you are flawed. You have not hidden it. That is your greatest gift to me.

—Alice Walker, *Possessing the Secret of Joy*

When I emerged from isolation in the spring of 2021, the first person I met with was my ninety-six-year-old mother. I got one of the earliest vaccinations available so I could visit her long-term care facility. I was looking forward to seeing her after so much had changed in my life. Due to the COVID-19 lockdown, we hadn't been able to meet since before I learned I had cancer.

As I walked down the hall to her room, I felt a childlike eagerness to catch sight of her, glad that my soft new hair was beginning to show so that my new appearance wouldn't startle her. During our separation we'd spoken on the phone, and I felt nourished by her affection and humor. But as soon as I walked in the door, seeing her for the first time, I realized something was wrong.

She acknowledged me with a nod, but there was no warmth in her face. I recognized that expression. She was angry. When my mother gets anxious, she covers it up with a prickly defense mechanism. But each time I'm stung by it, it feels like the first time.

I took off my coat and sat down to listen. It felt as though I'd arrived in the second act of a drama, but I tried to make sense of the story. She was accusing the housekeeper of stealing a teacup. Before we could have a mother-daughter reunion, I knew I had to give her space to de-escalate. But her anger became more intense. "I want to wring her neck!" That phrase triggered early memories. I felt like a three-year-old whose loving mother had disappeared, replaced by Cinderella's wicked stepmother.

MELTING INTO GRACE

I was almost sucked into my core fear, a feeling that I was unworthy of my mother's love, but something unexpected happened instead: a spontaneous burst of compassion and clarity. The intensity of my mother's rage along with my disappointment melted my three-year-old self into an open space of unconditional compassion.

I felt as though I was giving birth to my mother, this beautiful, innocent baby, holding her with a powerful energy that flowed between us.

I leaned forward and I held her hands and gazed into her eyes. I said, "Mum, this missing teacup represents the pain of everything you've lost. And you've lost so much. I was with you the night that you started choking and we called the ambulance. They took you to the hospital and you never went home again. That night, your world disappeared: your home, your routine, all your reference points. You lost your neighborhood, your backyard, your history. And when you wake up in the morning, you remember that all your friends have died. Mum, you've suffered so much. You've lost your power."

I felt my mother's grief and saw how her life had been shaped by the core fear that she was unlovable. She'd been a neglected child searching for a love that would confirm her worthiness. But her prickly defenses triggered the opposite response to the one she was so hungry for.

I saw all of this in a grace-filled moment of unconditional love. Simultaneously I realized that I too had misunderstood the meaning of love, thinking it was something I needed to receive to become complete. Now it was in reverse. Leaning forward, holding my mother's hands and looking into her eyes, I told her that she was my hero, that she had always deserved to be loved.

She started to cry, which is rare. When she's vulnerable, she normally makes people back away. But this time I was leaning forward, speaking her truth to her, and she was nodding. She quietly said, "Yes."

The story of the housekeeper stealing something was just a package for her suffering—a package that could have easily been undelivered if I'd taken it at face value, as I often do.

I'm grateful that this healing happened. My mother and I have had a difficult relationship in the past, but now I feel that we can enjoy the last chapter of our life together without regrets.

The love between us was like a mother and child in reverse. It broke the shell around both of our hearts at the same time, touching and healing the wound of our core fears. Out came our soft innocence welcoming this vulnerable new person when she showed up. And she, at last, was the mother I always knew was there.

THE IMPACT OF HELPING VERSUS HARM

When I said goodbye to my mother that day, I was crying. It was as though I felt our separation for the first time. It was different from past times when that aloneness felt like abandonment. This time it was my mother's story, not my own.

I imagined how, as a child, she was unable to tolerate isolation, so she protected herself by going numb. How she took refuge in frozen fear by becoming the perfect housewife and mother, all the while feeling invisible. How her rage would burst out in ways no one could sympathize with. And how, at age ninety-six, she might finally be open to love.

I cried with gratitude that having composted the suffering of my life story, I was able to offer understanding and comfort to hers.

FLIPPING THE SCRIPT

Compassion doesn't always arise spontaneously. Most of the time we need to actively reverse our habits of thought by training our mind. In the Buddhist tradition, *lojong*, or mind-training, is essential to stabilize the qualities of an open heart. To close this chapter, here is an adapted form of lojong[7] that we can use to "flip the script" of frozen fear with the four compassionate powers of tenderness, sadness, mercy, and fearlessness.

Interrupting Complaint with Tenderness: From "Why?" to "Why Not?"

"Why does this always happen to me?" The first practice is to arouse the power of compassion to tenderly be present with the suffering of impermanence. My doctor supported me to stay present with the shock of sudden change: "I see you, I'm here with you." This is what enabled me to pay her kindness forward and offer tender presence to my mother, to see her fear underneath her story about the housekeeper.

Our first challenge is to flip the script that says things should remain the same: "This shouldn't be happening," or "What did I do to deserve this?" With tenderness, when we hear this complaint in our mind, we refocus our attention toward the original wound, as I did with my mother and as Antoinette did with Michael. The truth of impermanence brings with it the grief of loss, which needs to be touched gently.

Melting Divisiveness with Sadness:
From Pointing to Them to "Just Like Me"

"We're different. There's not enough to go around, and we need it more than they do." The habit of dividing "us" from "them" runs deep. The teachings on bodhicitta invite us to consider this barrier as frozen fear. It not only cuts us off from others, but it also blocks us from our own heart and humanity. Whenever we notice divisiveness arising in our thoughts or words, we can practice touching that barrier with sadness and flip the script.

My mother saw the housekeeper as a thief, but I knew she was innocent. We can't see reality clearly through the filter of divisiveness. It distorts our view of not only others but also ourselves.

The practice of lojong can give us insight into poverty mentality, the illusion of being cut off that makes us want to hoard goodness on our side, inflating our value at someone else's expense. Seeing this with the compassionate power of sadness equalizes the value of self and others. We restore the supply chain of interdependence when we rehumanize the other person by flipping the script: "Just like me, Mum, the housekeeper is doing her best to make you happy." We're all in this together.

Breathing In Blame with Mercy:
From "All Your Fault" to "No Fault"

"Look at what she did to me. I can't let her get away with that." Here, let's investigate the habit of blame. Where does blame come from and what is the effect on our relationships? Blame inflames conflict instead of resolving it. We toss the hot potato of blame toward someone when we're afraid that owning it would prove we're unforgivable. The third compassionate power—mercy—sees that there's no basis for this fear. Absorbing blame with mercy opens the door to reconciliation and heals the fabric of relationship. This isn't about self-denigration, nor is it blocking a pathway to justice. It is simply a human gesture for opening our heart.

When we as a listener absorb the blame rather than buying into it, we're doing it to create space in the relationship. By flipping the script from blame to mercy, we can melt aggression on the spot.

Fearlessly Saying No to Retaliation: From "Get Even" to "Working It Out"

"He deserves to hurt as much as he's hurt me." Lojong teachings can also be applied to flip the script when we wish harm another. Retaliation is the final stage of hate speech, whether in our mind or in our spoken words. It is spun with stories that justify causing harm to the person or group of people we've targeted. When my mother wanted to wring the neck of her housekeeper, she was enacting a projection of the part of herself that she believed should be punished. When I heard my mother say this, I winced, envisioning all the innocent people who've been literally lynched by hatred.

The logic of hate speech tells us that punishing someone for our real or imagined suffering will bring relief. But is that true? Softening our heart, we might find the thread of retaliation going back to meeting our own pain with "What did I do to deserve this?" The hidden fear and false belief is "I must have done something to deserve this." Fearlessly cutting through this logic, we can see that retaliating against others is rooted in wanting to punish them for our own pain. By retraining our minds with bodhicitta, we can uproot this link between suffering and punishment. Fearlessly flipping the script on hatred brings us home to the truth that suffering is as inevitable as the turning of the seasons. We can't blame winter for being cold. There's no need to take it personally. We don't relieve our pain by harming others.

Contemplation

FLIPPING THE SCRIPTS

- Training our mind in bodhicitta is the practice of meeting our confused ideas and flipping them. Reflect on and write examples from your personal experience of flipping these four scripts:
  - Interrupting complaint with tenderness: From "Why me?" to "Why not me?" Flipping from complaint to acceptance.
  - Melting divisiveness with sadness: From pointing to them to "just like me." Flipping from "me first" to "we together."
  - Breathing in blame with mercy: From "all your fault" to "no fault." Flipping from blame to mercy.
  - Fearlessly saying no to retaliation: From "get even" to "working it out." Flipping from wanting to punish to fearlessly opening your heart.

Meditation

COMPASSIONATELY MELTING SELF-AGGRESSION

10 MINUTES

In this meditation, we bring compassionate presence to our inner habit of bypassing pain with aggression. By recognizing these four kinds of self-aggression, we can interrupt them and give birth to love instead of fear.

Recognize the seeds of self-aggression when they show up as complaint. Let's take a simple example: On vacation you sprain your ankle and hear yourself saying, "This shouldn't be happening! Why me? Why now?"

Interrupting complaint with tenderness, from "Why me?" to "Why not me?": Listen to yourself with tender presence. Take a deep breath and open to both the original pain in your ankle and the aggression toward your own suffering.

Imagine being your own unconditionally loving healer, touching your pain with love. Extend your hands to that suffering and embrace it to your heart. With the out-breath, feel the compassionate power of tender acceptance.

Melting divisiveness with sadness, reconnecting with pain: Next, flip the script of divisiveness into sadness, embracing the pain in your ankle and letting it highlight the way aggression cuts us off from our own heart. Feeling this sadness, imagine that you are touching all the walls of frozen fear, the inhumane ways that we divide ourselves from whatever or whomever we feel threatened by.

Extend your arms as if touching that wall around your heart is touching all the walls that divide us. Breathe in the suffering of divisiveness and all the rhetoric of "us and them," opening to this great sadness and letting it dissolve in your heart. On the out-breath, imagine all the walls dissolving into compassion.

Breathing in blame with mercy, from "all your fault" to "no fault": Now, breathe in blame with mercy: "It's my fault, I should have worn my hiking boots instead of sandals."

(continued)

This may not sound like hate speech, but the habit of finding fault freezes compassion into blame. Blaming ourselves or blaming others diverts our attention from embracing pain with compassion. Instead, be merciful when we hear our inner voice of self-blame.

Extend your arms with the out-breath and touch the frozen fear of self-blame. Embrace it into your heart and dissolve the fear of being unforgivable. Rest in the compassionate power of mercy.

Fearlessly saying no to retaliation, from "get even" to "working it out": Self-aggression is based on the false idea that pain is a form of punishment that we somehow deserve. For example, instead of comforting ourselves with a change of plan, sitting on a sunny patio with an ice pack on our ankle or reading a new book, we might spend the day angry at ourselves, overeating or drinking in a downward spiral of punishment masked as a reward.

With compassion, extend your hands on the out-breath and touch the part of yourself that interprets pain as punishment. Fearlessly say "No!" to cut the narrative of self-retaliation. Cut through all the ways you've reacted to your suffering by hurting yourself. Compassionately bring your hands to your heart, bringing that lost child home. Dissolve into the limitless tenderness of your heart. On the out-breath, relax into the freedom of your basic innocence and goodness.

21

Joy

Chanting this cry is a way to rouse your head and shoulders, a way to rouse a sense of uplifted dignity. It is also a way to invoke the power of windhorse and the energy of basic goodness. We might call it a battle cry, as long as you understand that this particular battle is fighting against aggression, conquering aggression, rather than promoting hatred or warfare. We could say that the warrior's cry celebrates victory over war, victory over aggression. It is also a celebration of overcoming obstacles. The warrior's cry goes like this: Ki Ki So So.

—Chögyam Trungpa, *Great Eastern Sun*

Sixteen sessions of radiation were a breeze compared to chemotherapy. When the final day came around at last, my treatment team congratulated me and asked if I had planned a special celebration. I hesitated at first, but then told them the truth: "I'm heading to a hospice to be with a friend who is dying today." What they couldn't possibly understand was that for me, the tender sadness of being with my friend was bearing witness not only to her passing but also to a celebration that it's possible to be reborn from fear into love.

When I first entered Jennifer's room a month earlier, we greeted each other like sisters, patting each other's soft growth of new hair. She recognized that I had a life force left in me that she lacked. I saw in her the unwaning elegance that I'd always admired. She had a sharp, biting intelligence. No nonsense or fluff, her clear eyes could look through to your soul. Our friendship was more spiritual than familiar, and my visits during the last few weeks of her life had a timeless quality of presence rather than looking back to her past or ahead to the shrinking days and hours that her body had left.

PURE REALMS

Jennifer and I talked about the Buddhist teaching that it's possible to be reborn into a kind of heaven after we die. It's called a "pure realm." In fact, there are many of these heavens to choose from depending on the aspirations we make in our lifetime. When we express a wish to be reborn in a pure realm, our intention isn't to live in eternal happiness. Rather, our motivation is to complete our training as a bodhisattva to benefit beings. So, these kinds of after-death heavens are temporary rather than eternal. A bit like vacationing in a beautiful resort to restore our health so that we can return to work.

Imagining what happens after death wasn't Jennifer's idea of a pure realm. Instead, she preferred to see the beauty and goodness of human society here and now. I saw in her the confidence that comes from melting the core fear of self-doubt into trust in basic goodness. As a spiritual warrior, she did her best to bring out these qualities in her everyday life.

Jennifer and I had been diagnosed with cancer at the same time the previous summer. But hers was pancreatic, with no hope of surviving even one year. She kept her diagnosis to herself for the first few weeks and quietly began the process of clearing space in her life to leave. She wanted to make one last work of art, a graceful white-marble sculpture to describe her vision of a human society liberated from fear. The stone seemed to be dancing, with soft winglike peaks reaching up to the sky. It represented a Buddhist *lhasang*, a joyful community gathering. Of all the spiritual practices we shared in our decades together, this was Jennifer's favorite.

LHASANG

Lhasang—from the Tibetan words *lha*, meaning "heaven"; and *sang*, meaning "to purify"—is a smoke offering, a celebratory ritual that's popular among the Himalayan people and given to Western Tibetan Buddhist students by our teacher Chögyam Trungpa Rinpoche. Juniper shrubs grow on mountains that seem to touch the sky, so juniper smoke is regarded as a sacred offering that joins heaven and earth. People gather in a circle around a blazing fire and make offerings and aspirations. The smoke goes up and blessings descend. The joyful proclamation is a mantra: KI KI SO SO! The purpose of a lhasang is to uplift our spirits, feel our connection to the natural world, and renew our confidence in the goodness of our relationships with one another.

Jennifer's vision of a lhasang extended to her final hours. Her friends chanted the mantra KI KI SO SO as she took her last breath. It felt as though her spirit dissipated into the sky like juniper smoke. Later that day, we gathered to welcome her body into our community shrine room. She rested there for hours, with a peaceful expression on her face, wearing the white gown she had chosen for the occasion. The space was powerful, full of warmth and gratitude. Her marble sculpture was in front of the shrine with incense smoke curling around it. The gift of this teaching on death was her final offering to our community.

Jennifer's passing was indeed a lhasang, earth reaching up and touching heaven. Outside the window, the cherry blossoms were beginning to bloom. In the distance, beyond the city skyline, the peaks of the North Shore Mountains were catching the late-afternoon light. "Yes," I thought, "this is what the blessings of basic goodness feel like. Jennifer's aspiration to be reborn into a pure realm has landed in our hearts here and now, in the beauty and magic of being together beyond the fear of death."

SEEING WITH FRESH EYES

Throughout this bardo journey, we have been exploring the relationship between love and fear in various ways. When we emerge from our personal crises into a new normal, we might look around at our world with fresh eyes, appreciating what it means to be alive. At the same time, we might notice the larger themes of love and fear as they play out in our families and communities. It's tempting to be lured into fear-based narratives that speak to us from the media, but just as we work with our own mind in meditation, we can unmask these narratives by grounding ourselves in the present moment, one breath at a time.

The lesson that Jennifer taught me was to keep coming back to the cultures of kindness in our human society and the power that comes from connecting to the earth as our collective body. These cultures communicate with the natural world in traditional rituals such as lhasang, folk dancing, or seasonal festivities. We need to lift up our gaze from our screens, look at the sky, and at the same time touch the earth beneath us. Enlightenment isn't some faraway experience that happens after we die. There is a pure realm here and now if we meet each moment of our life, as well as our last breath, with love. The way to do this is to take time throughout our day to pause, interrupt whatever we're doing, and just feel our humanity; feel that we belong here on this earth. Feel your heart, take a deep breath, and open. Let your identity dissolve into your breath. Look up and let go into the sky. That's all. Then return to whatever comes next.

Contemplation

RITUALS FOR DYING

- Reflect on your personal family history and culture. What were the community rituals and folk dances that were celebrated? Imagine the effect they might have had on the community and write your thoughts about this.
- What were the funeral traditions practiced in the past in your family culture? What traces of these practices remain today? Imagine the effect those traditions might have had for a family and write your thoughts about it.

Meditation

AROUSING COURAGE

5 MINUTES

In this meditation, we envision the joyful practice of lhasang as joining heaven and earth within our own body and home environment. We can enhance this by burning incense or placing a few grains of dried juniper or cedar on a burning charcoal to create a column of smoke.

(continued)

Sit in an upright posture, imagining your body to be like a mountain.

Feel the top of your head like the peak, touching the sky.

Feel your shoulders and chest open and uplifted, like alpine meadows.

Feel your heart as limitless space, big enough for all humanity to meet in joyful celebration.

Feel the weight of your lower body anchored to the earth, with your spine strong as an oak tree.

Joyfully chant KI KI SO SO! As the smoke curls up, giving voice to the best of intentions, the wish to strengthen the cultures of love, beauty, and goodness in our world.

Repeat this three times, taking your time to feel the energy in your body.

Rest in silence, imagining the blessings of our ancestor warriors descending into your body and home.

At the conclusion, dedicate your meditation with the intention to see your body, your home, and your world as sacred, full of blessings. Celebrate the melting of core fear into this vision of our basic goodness.

22

Rebirth

The world has order and power and richness that can teach you how to conduct your life artfully, with kindness to others and care for yourself.

—Chögyam Trungpa, *Shambhala:*
The Sacred Path of the Warrior

On the first day of a watercolor painting class, gathering my art supplies, I found myself feeling like a child on the first day of school. It was July 2021, my official reentry to the world I had left behind a year earlier. I finally had enough hair to pass as a normal healthy woman, but I felt self-conscious, my new body image still unfamiliar. I had to keep reminding myself that the cancer-treatment bardo was over.

When I walked into the classroom, we were allowed to remove our masks. It was the first time I could see and chat with people. They knew nothing about my last year, and I knew nothing about theirs. But we had the shared experience of pandemic isolation. What used to be ordinary was now extraordinary. I looked at each face as if being reunited with a long lost relative. I wanted to absorb every detail as we chatted with each other.

It was a small class, nine people in a room with windows looking out over a garden. The teacher introduced herself. "Good morning!

My name is Sonja, and I'm excited that we can finally meet in person."

Sonja had a passion for art that felt almost reverential. She restrained my impulse to splash color onto the page like a crossing guard protecting children on the road. It was as if she was saying: "Wait a minute; don't be in such a hurry! Stop, look, and pay attention."

For the first hour of class, one step at a time, she helped us make a relationship with the qualities of paper, pencils, eraser, palette, paints, and brushes. It was as though she brought these inanimate objects to life.

We listened attentively to Sonja's instructions, then we worked in silence, mixing the colors of our palettes, dipping our brushes, then gently touching down on the blank paper, an open space with infinite possibilities. I held my breath as my brush made the first dot of color, then I relaxed as it swept like a dancer in a small, graceful arc. I had no idea what would happen next, but I trusted that whatever emerged would have its own beauty—a fresh start.

As the day went on, my classmates and I would occasionally get up to stretch our legs, pausing to look at one another's work. The comments we made were unconditionally encouraging: "Really nice; I like the way you blended those colors." It was clear that some were more skilled than others, but Sonja's enthusiasm for learning was contagious. There was no such thing as mistakes; only feedback from the paper and brush. I couldn't have planned a better way to celebrate my rebirth into a new normal.

NEW NORMAL

As bardo warriors, we can discover that there's joy and creativity on the other side of fear. We've learned to live in an upside-down world, to meet and melt our fear with compassion. When we walk back into what seems like normal life, we're forever changed—and that's a good thing. Yes, there may be scars and some open wounds yet to heal, but if we've learned to be grateful for each moment, to feel affection for our life and our world, we've learned the most important lesson.

What we learn about fear from one bardo will soften and strengthen us for the next. If we know how to nourish our body with beauty, our heart with wisdom, and our mind with space, we can liberate ourselves from fear like a mother bringing her lost child home.

CLOSING DEDICATION

When our bardo comes to an end and we're giving birth to our new normal, love restores genuine confidence in our goodness. We're okay, we're basically good. This isn't a one-time event. It's an embracing, turning toward that fear many times and bringing it to our heart.

For those of you reading this bardo guide to meet the challenges of change in your life, I hope that you're inspired by these teachings and that you can find spiritual friends to accompany you on this path. We are working our way through extremely difficult challenges. These profound teachings have been with us for thousands of years and yet, because they point to the truth of our human heart, they are completely fresh and totally necessary in the world today.

When our bardo has ended and we've settled into a new life, our practice of opening our heart continues. We're sensitive to the suffering of others and look for ways to be of help. We want to nourish them with beauty, love, and wisdom so that their rude awakenings will be protected. We pay attention to the everyday exchanges that melt the barriers between us. Let's keep this aspiration alive by walking through our life a little more slowly, feeling the flow of kindness as the invisible power that can restore trust in the goodness of our humanity during difficult times.

Thank you for your patience and exertion and for your loving-kindness to meet whatever is arising in your experience—the sadness, pain, and joy. Welcome and create space to simply be with what is and keep supporting and helping one another so that we can really make the best use of this life for the benefit of others.

Contemplation

BEAUTY AND RESILIENCE

- Here is a self-reflection based on the words of my teacher Chögyam Trungpa: "The best of human life can be realized under ordinary circumstances. In this world, as it is, we can find a good and meaningful human life that will also serve others. That is our true richness."[8] There are daunting crises in the world today, but there is also beauty and resilience. Our strength comes from meeting the everyday challenges in our life with an open mind, tender heart, and mindful presence. What have you learned about your inner richness and strength?
- How has your bravery in the face of fear been a gift to others?
- Consider writing yourself a thank-you letter for the courage and inspiration you've brought to this bardo journey.

Meditation

BENDING IN THE WIND

10 MINUTES

As our last meditation in this journey together, here is a practice for meeting the upcoming bardos we and others will face in our lives. It is an aspiration prayer, setting an intention to be of benefit.

Sit in a comfortable position and, if you like, place one or both hands over your heart. Repeat these aspirations to yourself or rewrite them in your own words:

May I nourish myself with beauty. May my body open to the energetic relationship that I have with the physical environment around me.

May my body dance with reality—the colors, fragrances, sounds, tastes, and sensations of my everyday experience—as a partner.

May I nourish my heart with wisdom. May I be sensitive, able to read the emotional energy of my relationships and intuitively respond to the needs of others in the same way as I would to myself.

May I nourish my mind with love. May I trust my curious, open mind, poised at the tipping point of not-knowing rather than being distracted by preconceived strategies.

Set your intention to create time to pause and rest often, every day, simply being with a feeling of your goodness, healthiness, kindness.

ACKNOWLEDGMENTS

Writing this book was a healing process that could never have happened without the support of many friends. In particular, the topic of the bardo originated from a class I was invited to teach for the Austin Shambhala Center. Karen Fitzsimmons generously transcribed those talks, and I was helped and encouraged along the way by my friends Mary Sehlinger, Dede and Bill Gaston, and Val Monroe. I also appreciated feedback from Greg Heffron's Green Zone group, especially Mary Bolton, Christine Behrens, Ida Linse, and Hilde Brune.

In the final stage of the project, Janet McKinley carefully read through the manuscript with an eye that I lacked for details. Silas Rosenblatt gave me a jump-start when I needed it and helped brainstorm the book's working title. Truly, I could never have completed this book without them, so I'm very grateful.

Every morning while I was writing, my husband, Jerry, delivered ginger tea, lemon water, and coffee to keep me going. Then in the afternoon, we walked in beautiful places, laughing often and easily. I couldn't have survived this journey without his loving support. I'm also blessed to have three amazing sisters whom I love dearly: Mary and Pamela, who are also breast cancer survivors, and Sheelagh, who helped me in many ways, from making sure I had a port catheter for my chemotherapy IVs to sending me knitted caps when I had no hair.

I want to also acknowledge the medical team who have been supporting my cancer recovery over the past couple of years, especially my family doctor, Bella Hughan, and my oncologist, Tamara Shenkier, along with dozens of nurses and technicians who are living examples of a culture of kindness. Most of all, I have no words to express the gratitude I feel for my Tibetan Buddhist teachers and the lineage of blessings they brought to Western students of my generation. Throughout the book, when I refer to *my teacher*, this could be any one of several great masters I've been fortunate to study with. Most often I'm referencing my root guru, Chögyam Trungpa Rinpoche. After his passing in 1987, I studied for twenty years with the mahamudra master Khenchen Thrangu Rinpoche, who guided me in the traditional three-year retreat and installed me as the *drupon*, or retreat director, for the next six years. I was fortunate to also mentor with Ani Pema Chödrön while at Gampo Abbey, and she continues to be my guide and inspiration on the path, along with my meditation instructor, John Rockwell. After leaving the abbey, I was grateful to study for a time with Trungpa Rinpoche's son, Sakyong Mipham Rinpoche, and to serve as an *acharya*, or senior teacher, for his community.

Finally, thank you to the friends who join me for morning meditation online. You've been my shelter in the storm.

I'd like to also express my gratitude to Shambhala Publications and my editor, Breanna Locke, for their trust, encouragement, and skills in bringing this project to completion.

NOTES

1. Susan Gillis Chapman, *The Five Keys to Mindful Communication: Using Deep Listening and Mindful Speech to Strengthen Relationships, Heal Conflicts, and Accomplish Your Goals* (Boulder, CO: Shambhala, 2012), 9–10.
2. Shambhala teachings on spiritual warriorship are explained in Chögyam Trungpa, *Shambhala: The Sacred Path of the Warrior* (Boston: Shambhala, 2015).
3. Gillis Chapman, *Five Keys to Mindful Communication*, 51–52.
4. Martin Luther King Jr., "Where Do We Go from Here?" (speech, Eleventh Annual Convention of the Southern Christian Leadership Conference, August 16, 1967, Atlanta, GA).
5. Gary Younge, "The Heroism of Antoinette Tuff Reveals What's Missing from Politics," *Guardian*, August 25, 2013, www .theguardian.com/commentisfree/2013/aug/25/antoinette-tuff-heroism-missing-from-politics.
6. Antoinette Tuff and Alex Tresniowski, *Prepared for a Purpose: The Inspiring True Story of How One Woman Saved an Atlanta School Under Siege* (Bloomington, MN: Bethany House, 2014), eBook.
7. For more formal teachings on the practice of lojong, see Chögyam Trungpa, *Training the Mind and Cultivating Loving-Kindness* (Boston: Shambhala, 2005); or Traleg Kyabgon, *The*

Practice of Lojong: Cultivating Compassion through Training the Mind (Boston: Shambhala, 2007).

8. Trungpa, *Shambhala*, 106.

INDEX

ABOUT THE AUTHOR

SUSAN GILLIS CHAPMAN is a retired couples and family therapist who has been studying, practicing, and teaching Buddhism and mindfulness meditation for fifty years. She is the author of *The Five Keys to Mindful Communication: Using Deep Listening and Mindful Speech to Strengthen Relationships, Heal Conflicts, and Accomplish Your Goals*. She lives in Burnaby, British Columbia, with her husband, Jerry, and their cat, Ziji. She has one adult son, Sheehan, and two stepdaughters, Sarah and Autumn. For more information, visit her website at www.susangillischapman.com.